The Eight Visits

Roland Merullo

The Eight Visits

ISBN: 979-8-9866266-6-6
Also available in eBook format

PFP Publishing
PO Box 102
Rockport, ME 04856

For Alexandra & Juliana

"Wisdom exalteth her children,
And layeth hold of them that seek her.
He that loveth her loveth life."

—The Apocrypha 4:11-12

My Dear Grandchild,

You haven't been born yet. There's a chance you'll never be born, though we have two daughters in their twenties, and both say they want to have children, so I think the chances of you showing up are pretty good. In fact, there may be more than one of you, so I should probably have addressed this to "My Dear Grandchildren." But I like to think of us as communicating one-to-one. I'm 70, and we had our daughters when I was 44 and 48 (Amanda—your grandmother—and I were married eighteen years before two spirits joined us here on this planetary adventure; she gave birth at 41 and 45) so, even if you and I actually meet in person, I'll probably depart for other adventures before you're old enough to talk about the things I'm writing here.

And what are those things? Well, things we probably don't talk about enough in our busy days: aspects of the interior life mostly, though each one of the visits described here is grounded in an exterior event. Those events come unembellished from my own life, which has been, so far at least, a truly wonderful life. Although, thankfully, I'm not wealthy, I did travel from the lower rungs of the American socio-economic ladder to the country's most elite schools. I spent years working in a region we used to call 'behind the Iron

Curtain', and months on a Pacific atoll with no electricity, running water, or medical care. I've had a great marriage—almost 45 years at this point—and with that amazing woman I raised two of the finest human beings I know. I've driven a Boston cab, worked for years as a carpenter, taught in college, and eventually—my great dream—made a living from writing novels. I've suffered, too, physically, mentally, psychologically—enough to instruct me without crushing me.

All of it's a lesson, that's what I believe. Everything that happens to us, good, bad, large and small, is a kind of teaching, and we can choose to learn from it or not, choose to say yes or no to it, choose gratitude or bitterness. I'm a hundred per cent sure your lessons will be different from mine, but maybe all our lessons lead in the same direction—toward humility and love and appreciation, so, as Walt Whitman said, "All I mark as my own, you shall offset it with your own/ Else it were time lost listening to me." I'll try, in this letter, to convey a piece of my experience of living, but, at the same time, please don't think of this as advice. It's a love letter across the generations. It's sincere and imperfect and quirky. Like me. Just ask your mother and your aunt.

A Little Explanation First

On eight occasions in my life so far, always at what would turn out to be critical moments—though they didn't always seem that way at the time—I was visited by a woman who called herself Elemosina (pronounced L—A—MOSE-ee-nah.) I say 'woman' but that term is misleading. It's better to describe Elemosina as a spirit, a *presence,* and while I've never seen her take human form—or any form, for that matter—there is the sense that she's female. I don't know how to explain that. Maybe it's the 'voice' with which she speaks to me, though it isn't really a voice at all but more like a brain-to-brain communication. That 'voice' sounds unlike any woman I've ever known or heard, and it's conveyed in a kind of transfer of mental energy rather than via sounds or syllables. But I have the sense when I hear it that I'm listening to a female spirit. I can't say that I see her. It's more that I know without any doubt that I'm in her presence. It's an odd feeling, as if I'm surrounded by a vapor that isn't recognized by any of my ordinary senses. I can't see this vapor, can't smell or taste it. I feel it, but not the way you feel cold or warmth against your skin. I feel it the way you feel affection for someone, the way you miss loved ones when they're gone, the way you experience fear or hope.

Each of these eight visits was different in location and timing, though somewhat similar in tone and content. I think of them as cumulative, so maybe you should read them with that in mind. It's only in looking back that I realize how important they were, that they were drawn from a well of wisdom we all share and to which we all have access. You might guess they were the usual big moments in a life: the day before leaving home for the first time, the day before getting married, the times my children were born, or when I had a severe illness and thought about dying. In some cases that would be true, but Elemosina's visits were subtle, unpredictable, and always grew from but transcended the exterior events themselves.

I've come to believe that we all have an Elemosina in our depths. For reasons I don't understand, not all of us realize that, not consciously, at least, or not yet. Not all of us hear what our guiding spirits are saying; perhaps because we don't take the time to listen. We don't drink from the well, or we don't believe the well is there.

A wine connoisseur can taste certain flavors in a glass of Barolo that the rest of us miss. A chef will identify ingredients in a stew that only some of us can taste and few of us can talk about intelligently. A meteorologist can see things in a weather pattern that I can't. A great guitarist can make sounds I could never make. For whatever reason, I happen to have the ability to 'hear' my Elemosina, to understand that I'm in her presence, and to remember the precise meaning of those visits, even many years later. It should go without saying that I don't think this ability makes me a better human being than anyone else. The accomplished guitarist isn't a better human being; he or she just plays the guitar better. And what a sad thing it would be if the guitarist didn't play, if the chef didn't cook, if the person who was drawn to be a meteorologist and spent decades developing those skills didn't use them.

So I've decided, after years of keeping these visitations private, to write this long letter to you about my moments with Elemosina, her eight (so far) visits. As she said to me several times, her communications are not just experiences. There's a purpose to them. She's always left it up to me to figure out what that purpose is, and I think, over these many years, I'm close to doing that. Maybe by setting these moments on the page I'll make that final step of understanding, but I worry that, once I get there, once I fully grasp the purpose of her mysterious visits, they'll stop happening and I'll be left to go through the rest of life without the great comfort of her wisdom.

I've never had any control over the timing, frequency, or duration of her visits, and they're rare. Eight in seventy years. It's not like they happen at regular intervals, and not like it would do any good for me to get down on my knees and ask for her to show up. One of the many gifts she's given me is a trust in my intuition. Over the years, with her encouragement, I've sharpened that tool, come to trust it more and more; I've seen the ways intuition can mislead a person, too, but I hope I've learned how to avoid those traps. My intuition tells me that now is the time to share this story with the spirit or spirits my daughters will bring into this world. So, to the best of my ability, I'll try to do that.

Here goes.

The First Visit
Losing Someone

Elemosina visited me for the first time when I was eleven years and nine months old. "Going on twelve" is how we used to say it, trying to grow up faster, as children often do. Having nothing with which to compare the experience of sensing Elemosina's presence and hearing her voice, I should probably have felt afraid on that first visit, or at least confused. But the truth is my main emotion was a mild surprise coupled with a sense of awe. A strange familiarity, too. There was something eerily recognizable about the four or five minutes she spent with me on that day. For many people, making love for the first time, exciting as it may be, carries with it that same subtle undercurrent of familiarity. It's possible death will feel that way, I don't know. To me, those are signs that our spirits have experienced those kinds of moments before, that we're separated from some vast and complicated other reality—an unimaginably long series of previous lives maybe—by only the thinnest of invisible membranes.

Both my father's parents—Joe and Eleonora—were immigrants, each of them born in tiny villages in the hills half an hour east of Naples, Italy. I've been fortunate enough to visit those villages more than once, including very recently, and it's not hard for me to imagine why my grandparents left. Southern Italy in the nineteenth and early twentieth century offered next to no chance of upward mobility. You were the person you were born as: no matter your ambition, skill, or effort, you remained in the social stratum of your parents.

Joe and Eleonora didn't know each other there, and sailed to America separately, making the rough crossing in steerage as youngsters, she in 1904 at the age of ten and he four years earlier at the age of thirteen. They met in Boston's North End, the city's Italian section, went through the usual courtship, were married a few miles north in the ethnically mixed enclave of Revere—countryside then. He worked as a tailor and she managed the household, cooked, cleaned, and raised five boys and three girls. The third of those children, and the first to graduate from high school, was my father. I had the great blessing to live upstairs from Joe and Eleonora until a month shy of my seventh birthday, at which point my parents built a house in the vacant lot next door, and we moved.

I saw my father's parents every day of my young life. They lived in a two-story red house with a gambrel roof (where they'd moved after the death, in childbirth, of my father's first wife and first child), and they had—by local standards—a large back yard. There were two different kinds of pear trees in that yard, two kinds of cherry trees, two plum trees, a peach tree, a grape arbor, eight feet tall, ten feet wide, and thirty feet long, and a garden thirty feet by a hundred, where Joe grew tomatoes, peppers, and eggplants. In one section of the basement they kept three large wine barrels—I can still see and smell them, all cobwebs and dust—and canning jars filled with vinegar peppers. There was a bocce court between the garden and the grape arbor, a dusty strip lined with old boards. I loved to watch my grandfather, father, and uncles play, and liked playing there with my two younger brothers, Steve and Ken. Every Sunday, one of Joe and Eleonora's children would come for the midday meal with their own spouse and children, and then, when the meal was finished, all the other children and spouses and kids would arrive and fill the house and yard. I had twenty-eight first cousins on that side of the family, fourteen aunts and uncles. I saw all of them every Sunday of my childhood, and on every holiday, and I could walk to every one of their houses in fifteen minutes or less.

On those Sundays the cousins would naturally break into groups according to age and play different kinds of games, or have different kinds of conversations. When we felt hungry, we'd climb the back steps, bang in through the screen door, swing by a table loaded with sandwiches, pies, cakes, and cookies, and receive hugs and kisses and handshakes from the aunts and uncles. What most other Americans call 'soda' or 'pop', we called 'tonic', and we were all served red wine at an early age and no fuss was made about that. Depending on our ages, our parents would mix different amounts of wine with orange tonic, which meant you could look around the table and tell the age of a cousin by the color of what she or he was drinking: the older ones' glasses would be purplish-red, the younger ones' a red-tinted orange.

My mother's family—her parents were immigrants from England—was quieter and less festive, though they all had great senses of humor, and those four grandparents formed a perfect balance for me: my grandmother on one side reciting poetry with a touch of British accent; and my grandmother on the other making simple, delectable meals of pasta and meatballs and the rolled, spiced beef called *braciole,* and the apple pies and Italian cookies, and small, honey-coated balls of fried dough called *strufoli.* My grandfather on one side teaching me to play chess, and my grandfather on the other teaching me to play bocce and the card game *briscola,* and a few words of his beautiful native language.

As I grew older, I'd walk down to my mother's parents' house on Wednesdays and earn a dime for carrying their trash barrels out to the sidewalk. Grandpa Haydock would play chess with me, taking his queen off the board at the start of each game until, eventually, I became good enough to play against him with even armies. Grandpa Merullo would pay me to catch the caterpillars that threatened his tomato crop. I'd kneel in the dirt and carefully inspect the plants, one by one, tracing the damage from the ground up, taking hold of a delicate, light-green leaf with thumb and index finger, gently turning it over and finding the red-spotted, horned green caterpillar there, munching away. Once I tracked down the caterpillar, I'd pinch off the leaf it was clinging to, and carry it over to my grandfather. He'd pay me according to the size: five or ten cents for the smaller creatures, up to a quarter for those who'd fattened themselves by eating a third of the greenery on a given plant, and even gnawing into the fruit. He'd tear a page from his newspaper, Boston's *Record American,* wrap it around the still-eating caterpillar, lay it on the concrete floor of the grape arbor, and light it on fire. Once he was sure the invader had perished, he'd stamp out the fire with his shoe. Why he didn't simply wrap up the caterpillar and stamp on the newspaper with his shoe, I never asked; his method didn't seem cruel to me then as it does now.

There's so much more I could say about that place and that childhood—the Coney-Island-like, three-mile strip of amusements a mile away at Revere Beach, the Little League games with fathers—some of them not quite sober—yelling encouragement to us from the amphitheater-shaped stands, the bare-knuckle fist-fights I saw and, for a short while, participated in, the hockey and touch football games in the narrow tar street in front of our house, the eccentric group of neighbors—nurses, factory workers, truck painters, laborers, plumbers, bookies—the church services and Mafia dens. . . but I want to talk about Elemosina's first visit, so I'll just leave the landscape of my earliest life sketched out in the few lines above.

I loved all four of my grandparents and was close to them, but I spent by far the most time with my father's father, Giuseppe, or, in America 'Joe.' I can calculate now that he turned seventy when I was 3 and living upstairs. My mother used to tell me that he and Eleonora would often come up just before bedtime so they could hold us for a few minutes, and I have an old photograph of Grandpa Merullo, the Italian patriarch, dressed in his white shirt and tailored trousers, balancing me on his lap and feeding me formula from a bottle. By the time I was of school age he'd retired from his tailor shop, so we passed many pleasant summer hours together, dealing with the caterpillars, wandering around the yard, playing cards in his kitchen, watching TV. Once, he took me on the subway into Boston to see the huge construction project we thought of then as 'urban renewal' that had devastated Scollay Square. A deep, ragged-edged, rectangular hole in the ground is what I remember, though I'd learn later that an entire vibrant neighborhood, Boston's West End, populated largely with immigrants, had been destroyed to make way for federal and state offices, and Boston City Hall—not long ago voted one of the country's ugliest buildings.

Joe was a thin, quiet man, nothing like the Italian stereotype. He didn't wave his arms and hands when he spoke. He ate in a delicate, reserved way. Bald on top, wearing eyeglasses with dark brown upper rims, always finely dressed, during thunderstorms he'd sometimes sit out at the edge of the grape arbor, in a metal lawn chair no less, and admire the bolts of lightning, while his wife and daughters screamed at him—Come inside, Pa! Joe, come in!—through the kitchen windows. I was his pal, and I can see now what having a young friend means to an elderly man who no longer heads off to work in the morning.

Joe had a troublesome heart, which, in a less dangerous way, I seem to have inherited. In the last few years of his life, on multiple occasions, I'd see an ambulance in front of the big red house on Essex Street, watch my grandfather being loaded into the back of it on a stretcher and carried away to one of the Boston hospitals. But he always returned. "The 'Iron Man of Mass General', they call him," my father used to say, proudly.

But then one summer it seemed that all those 'cardiac events' as we call them now, all those trips to the hospital, finally caught up with him. A hush fell over the red gambrel. I was eleven, living next door, and could feel it. My grandmother was praying constantly, my grandfather was spending a large part of every day lying on the sofa in the narrow TV room, talking less than usual, eating very little. Late one June afternoon, dressed in my Orioles uniform before an under-the-lights Little League game, I went over to visit him, knelt down beside the sofa so my face was close to his, and promised I'd get a hit for him. I remember the promise, but I don't remember what he said. No doubt he put a hand on my arm or head or let me kiss him—we were so comfortable with physical contact in that family—and nodded and thanked me, or said that a hit would surely make him feel better.

Charlie Anderson was pitching that night. Charlie

had the fiercest curveball in the league, but he threw it all the time, and I'd figured out that, if I just had the courage to stand there as the ball came toward my shoulder, it would curve in over the plate. That's what happened. I stood there as the ball came toward me, watched it start to curve. I swung and hit a triple down the left-field line. I remember standing, out-of-breath and happy, on the third-base bag, already anxious to tell my grandfather that I'd kept my promise, anxious to see if my triple off Charlie Anderson would help him feel better.

It was early June. We were still in school. And school for my two younger brothers and me—sixth grade, third grade, first grade—meant dressing in nice clothes, having our hair neatly combed and sprinkled with Vitalis, keeping a clean white handkerchief in our back pants pocket, and walking together every morning the few hundred yards up Essex Street to the Cassandra M. Barrows Elementary School, built in 1898.

But on that day, instead of having our Cream of Wheat and walking out the door, we were told to wait. "Your father has something to tell you," our mother said, without making eye contact. Our father hadn't been at the breakfast table, which was unusual. We heard him come down the stairs and then he sat in one of the kitchen chairs, but in a way that allowed us to stand in front of him, with our backs to the table. My mother stood behind him, wringing her hands. Something was wrong with our father's face; it was moving around, twitching, as if he were about to burst out laughing, but it didn't feel like a happy moment. My brothers and I stood in a row, shoulder-to-shoulder, just in front of him like lieutenants before a general, dressed for school, confused.

"God called Grandpa last night," was the first thing my father managed to say, after struggling for a few seconds.

We had no idea what he was talking about. Behind him, my mother, now with her hands clasped in front of her throat, seemed to be urging us to understand. We didn't understand.

"God called Grandpa," Pa repeated, and now he seemed to be crying, something we'd never seen. The muscles of his face were trembling and I was beginning to be able to guess what he meant and I could feel my whole body shaking. But we only looked at him, waiting, frightened at the sight of our parents in postures we'd never seen before.

"What do you mean, Pa?" I said, the oldest son, speaking for the three of us.

And finally, these words—"Grandpa died last night"—came out of his mouth and he burst into tears, and my mother burst into tears, and my brothers and I burst into tears, too, and stood there weeping, as if we understood that the blessed innocence of our childhood had been taken from us overnight.

We cried and hugged each other for a few minutes, and then my parents told us we had to go to school. This seemed a second cruelty. We resisted for a short while, then relented, went out the door, out of our yard, and onto the sidewalk, all of us still crying. Not many young boys, not many young boys in places like Revere at least, want classmates to see them crying. I remember, at one point, as we climbed the gentle rise toward the top of Essex Street, that I handed my handkerchief to my middle brother—who would one day become a street-fighter and then a Marine—so his friends wouldn't see him with tears on his face.

All the aunts, uncles, and cousins came to my grandparents' house that afternoon, and the kitchen and yard were festivals of weeping. Aunts keened in the kitchen. The smaller cousins wandered around under the grapevine, sad and confused. Neighbors and family friends brought plates of food—that was the tradition. I stayed in the yard for a while, and then, drawn by some instinct I could never have explained, left the comfort of that sorrowful group and walked up the street. Barrows School was a brick building, broader than it was tall, constructed as if to withstand an assault of nuclear missiles, three stories, thick redbrick walls and huge screened windows with concrete lintels. There was a dusty playground out front on the south side—the boys' side—and a set of thirty wide, concrete stairs, bracketed by boxy abutments, that led to a pair of wooden doors so heavy the younger kids couldn't pull them open.

I climbed halfway up those stairs and sat, looking across Mountain Avenue at the humble wood frame houses there. They were set close together behind cheap fences and tattered shrubs, looking still and at peace, as if nothing in the world had changed. After a time I lowered my head into my hands and cried for a minute or two, images of my grandfather parading across my brain: Joe sitting at the kitchen table in his white dress shirt, the brown-rimmed eyeglasses perched on the bridge of his small nose; Joe tossing the bocce ball underhanded and watching as it rolled along the dirt court and gently tapped his opponent's ball off to the side and nestled itself close against the small ball they called the *pallino;* Joe's spotted old hands dealing the cards in a game of *briscola* played on the plastic table cloth; Joe walking around the backyard with me and pointing up to the airplanes as they came in for a landing at Logan; Joe striding in his erect, old-man's posture up Essex Street to play cards with his friends at the Club, another redbrick building, flat-roofed, that occupied the lot beside our school. I sat there, a hundred feet away, and couldn't make myself look at it.

And then I 'heard' a voice. 'Heard' in quotes because, as I said, it was not exactly a voice and most likely wouldn't have been audible to someone sitting beside me. But it was clear and resonant, a woman's voice, but in a certain tone that was unlike any tone that had come from the mouths of my mother, aunts, or girl cousins. I sometimes think that, if there is a God, and if we do hear His or Her words after we die, they will sound like that voice, have the same authority, the same kindliness, the same intimacy and mystery.

Hard, isn't it? the voice said, quietly.

I was slightly startled, but not afraid. I opened my eyes—I can remember looking down at my Jack Purcell sneakers, at the dirt-stained laces, at the gritty concrete of the stair between them, but I was, as the saying goes, all ears. I nodded.

Everyone around you is sad, crying, calling his

name.

I nodded again.

And that makes you even sadder. Everyone is saying your grandfather is up in heaven now, playing cards with friends who've died, embracing his parents, happy, at peace. But his body is at the funeral home and will be buried in a casket in a few days, so what part of him is up in heaven? Have you wondered? Can his body be in two places at once, in the casket and in heaven? Do you believe it's the body he had as an old man, his head bald, teeth yellowed, the skin of his face wrinkled? Or is it the body he had when he was a boy, or a young man? You've seen the photos: Handsome, full of energy and hope. Twenty, thirty, thirty-five?

There was a pause then. I didn't move, didn't change my posture, and didn't even attempt to answer the questions. My fingers were in my thick black hair, my face pointed downwards, eyes open, throat half-closed. Waiting for more.

You loved him, the voice said. *What does that mean? That you liked being near him, liked the sound of his voice, the way he reached out and pulled you against him with one arm, the way he let you kiss his cheek, the gifts he gave you? The quarters held out to you after you'd caught a large caterpillar? The way he made you stand on a small stool and marked the bottoms of your trouser legs with the edge of a thin piece of soap when he was tailoring your Easter suits? The way he held the pins between his lips and then took them out one by one and pinned up the cuffs just so? The sound of his sewing machine when he was sitting there working?*

I started to cry again, because I understood that all that was gone now. The grumble of the sewing machine, the touch of his hands, the look in his brown eyes when he saw me step through the back door—it had disappeared overnight. For a fairly long stretch there was only silence, as if the woman who'd spoken was allowing me time to cry or to stop crying and gather myself. And, in fact, she didn't speak again until the crying eased. I sniffed, swiped at my eyes, then sat there quietly, waiting lips shaking but my body very still.

It's good to be sad, the voice said. *It's normal. Let yourself cry. Don't be ashamed of it. Your father cried. All your aunts, uncles, and cousins cried. Your grandmother will be crying for a long time now. . . . And, if you want to, let yourself imagine your grandfather as you remember him, only up in heaven, happy, playing cards with his friends. That image is comforting. . . .But the real truth is, your grandfather and his body were not the same thing, just as you and your body are not the same thing. Try to remember that as you grow older. You will have pain and injury and illness, but in those moments, try to say "I am not this body," and reach down into yourself for the place that is the Divine You. That part, the Divine You, your Essence, is very real, and your body is only a temporary vehicle for it. A disguise. A car carrying it down a long, winding road.*

Now, try to imagine that Divine You connecting with your grandfather's Divine You. That connection is love. It is eternal. Around it, shapes change, bodies change, as if you're looking into a kaleidoscope like the one he gave you for your fifth birthday. A circus of images. When you attend Mass, look up at the stained-glass windows, the paintings above the altar, the altar itself with its swirls of stone and gold-trimmed cloth, the marble blocks in the walls—one of them has your grandparents' names etched onto it because, like hundreds of other immigrants from Italy, they gave money to have that beautiful church built—the red carpet up the center aisle, the chandeliers, the ornate pulpit. Look at all those things and remember they're just decoration, merely part of something larger. They hint at the Great Truth, but are not its essence. Your feelings in that building, the sense you sometimes have of a world beyond the decorations, beyond the body, beyond the things you hope for and worry about—that, too, is part of the Divine You. In another few days, when you step into that church for your grandfather's funeral, look at all the beauty, the flowers, the women's hats, the men's suits, the marble, your cousins' faces, and remember to try and see all of it as decoration, the set of an elaborate play, and remember that your body is just a disguise that's constantly changing, a whirl of cosmic dust spun into a shape that moves and grows and, eventually, disappears. Do you understand?

Caught in the spell cast by her voice, I nodded, but I didn't really understand, not then at least, not at all.

Good, she said. *I am called Elemosina, and from time to time I will speak to you like this. The times when I'm not speaking, I'm close to you, always. We have that connection, you and I, just as you had with your Grandpa. Everyone on Earth has a connection like that, a guide, an advisor. But some people don't listen. Now go back and hug your grandmother and tell her you love her, and remember these things that I have said to you. Try always to remember them.*

I waited, hoping the spell would go on, dreading the return to Twenty Essex Street. When I understood that Elemosina would say nothing more, I looked up. For just an instant then the houses across the street, small and humble, standing there behind their chain-link and picket fences, messy shrubs and tiny lawns, seemed to be looking back at me. Decorations on something impossible to understand. The set of a play. The background of a painting. Without meaning to, I smiled, and then, after a few seconds, they were just houses and shrubs and fences again, and I stood up and walked down the concrete steps, across the dusty playground, across Mountain Avenue, and down the sidewalk of Essex Street. Near the bottom, I turned right, into the concrete walk that ran along the south side of my grandparents' house, and I climbed the steep set of brown wooden stairs and went in through the back door with the oval window at its center. My grandmother was sitting at the kitchen table with my aunts, crying, and she had a loop of rosary beads and large blue and white handkerchief clutched in both hands in her lap. I went over and hugged her and told her I loved her, and she reached up with one hand and pressed my face against her neck and held me that way. For a moment I thought about telling her what had just happened. I thought of repeating Elemosina's words, but I didn't do that.

"Eat, Rolly, eat something," one of my aunts said. I grabbed a cookie from a plate on the table, kissed my aunt on the way out the door, and went down into the yard to be with the cousins I loved.

The Second Visit
Finding Someone

Well, my dear grandchild, the description of Elemosina's second visit is going to follow the iceberg model: not much happened in the visible, tangible, above-the-surface world, but a lot happened to me in the interior, invisible world. At the time of the events described here—if they can even be called 'events'—I really had no idea what was going on, and certainly had no idea where they would lead. It's always that way, of course: only in hindsight can we see the interconnectedness of things, which is, I suppose, why I felt I had to wait until I turned 70 to write this. By that, I don't mean to say you won't understand anything that happens until you get old. Not at all! Only that from this vantage point there seem to be patterns to things, and I never saw those patterns when I was immersed in them.

What I find fascinating is that Elemosina—who is supposed to represent a kind of celestial wisdom; how else can I describe that?!—seemed to exist in a realm beyond time, a dimension where 'she' had access to what we think of as the future. I sometimes wish I could have understood that and listened to her with more trust, but there's the whole point: I wasn't then the person I am now, any more than the carrot seed is the carrot. In order for that seed to break open and flourish, there has to be sun and rain and time. Same with us, I think. There has to be pleasure and difficulty and time, and it's gradual, cumulative, as slow, in the larger picture, as the growth of a carrot is in the smaller.

Anyway, here's the story of her second visit.

As I bet you know by now, besides the pure enjoyment factor, playing a sport can offer a lot of value to the interior world: confidence, humility (it's so hard to lose, and such a good lesson), discipline, appreciation of the body, the joy of teamwork.

Your grandmother and I both played varsity sports in college (soccer for her and rowing for me), and our daughters played soccer, tennis, golf, and softball competitively, so I wouldn't be surprised if you're playing one kind of sport or another at this stage of your life, enjoying it, learning from it. (I'd call that 'spiritual' learning, but I use that loaded word carefully, and in a way that has little to do with organized religion.) Some people have zero interest in, and/or zero aptitude for sports, and find similar enjoyment in playing music, gardening, cooking, or the pursuit of other passions. Those passions often lead us to friendships and even love relationships, connections that seem to have happened by accident, but I think it's all part of the great tapestry of humanity, and in this troubled world we should consider ourselves very fortunate if we have enough time and energy left over after feeding, clothing, and housing ourselves to have the kind of fun that hobbies and passions offer.

I have other hobbies and other passions, but sports—rowing in particular—played a big role in my younger days.

If you live near a body of fresh water, a wide river or large enough lake, especially one near a college or private high school, you've likely seen a rowing team practicing, the long sleek boats moving across the surface in what appears an easy rhythm. But rowing, sometimes also called 'crew', is actually a grueling sport, as much about enduring pain as it is about technique or strength (though height and leg strength in particular do matter). The spring college races are typically 2,000 meters, and the exertion involved is the equivalent of lifting a 55-pound weight from the floor over your head, 36 times a minute for six minutes, in perfect unison with seven other people.

I spent my first two years of college at Boston University, then transferred to Brown, and rowed varsity crew at both places. Looking back on that experience, I see that my relationship to the sport was actually an introduction to aspects of life that are totally unconnected to crew, as if the oars and shells and the countless hours of practice in heat and cold, rain, snow, and sleet, were keys to doors that opened into strange rooms where I would end up wandering around for decades.

Elemosina's second visit was intricately tied to my time on three rivers: the Exeter River in New Hampshire, the Charles in Boston, and the Seekonk in Rhode Island.

I attended Revere, Massachusetts, Public Schools from first through eighth grades and was entirely happy for the first six years and utterly miserable for the last two. A strange occurrence—the Hand of Fate, I believe—led to my escaping that misery, and also led me onto those rivers.

My father had been a city councilor before I was born, and had remained active in local politics and community events. From time to time he'd attend meetings and civic dinners and basically drag my mother along—she was much less comfortable in social situations. At the close of one of those functions, a woman my mother didn't know well, but recognized, approached her and said, "Are you Rolly Merullo's mother?" No doubt my mother worried the woman was going to report me for some transgression of local etiquette, or worse, but, after a slight hesitation, she admitted that she was, in fact, Rolly Merullo's mother. That took courage! The woman then spoke words that seem incredible to me now, and that my mother relayed to me only when I was in my fifties: "You have to get him out of here."

"What do you mean?" My mother asked.

"You have to get him out of this school system and into a private school."

"We don't have the money for that," my mother said.

"You don't have to have the money," the woman told her. "*The schools* have the money. He could get a scholarship. You have to get him out of here."

It strikes me now, as a longtime father, that approaching another parent and saying something like "You have to get your child out of here," is an act that could be considered at least odd and more likely offensive. Maybe my mother waited all those years to tell me the story because, at the time, she was intimidated or insulted, or even angry. I don't know.

But the advice—an exhortation, really—must have reached her at some level. She told me she went home and thought about the prospects of getting me into a private school, but had no idea how to go about it. She knew the woman's name, looked it up in the phone book, dialed her number, and said, "This is Eileen Merullo, Rolly's mother. You told me to try to get him into a private school, but I don't know how to do that."

The woman said, "You go to the library and look up private schools and you write them a letter asking for an application form."

My mother found the book at the Revere Public Library and sent handwritten letters to twenty private schools, names we'd never heard spoken in our provincial world of Sunday gatherings and street sports. Phillips Exeter, Phillips Andover, Choate, Milton Academy, Hotchkiss, St. Paul's, St. Mark's, Groton, Loomis Chafee. I remember a stack of twelve or fifteen school catalogues on the dining room table. I filled out the applications, took the necessary SSAT exam at Boston Latin School, and, a few months later, was accepted everywhere I'd applied.

I don't take too much credit for those acceptances. School had always come easy for me, in part because my mother read to me from the time I was very young. Multiple-choice examinations came easily, also, which is a good talent to have but hardly a true measure of intelligence. The key factor, most likely, was that, in those long-ago days, elite private schools like the ones mentioned above received very few applications from the Reveres of this world, and from the children of families like ours. My mother was the only person on our crowded street with a college education, the only one of my many aunts and uncles who'd earned a four-year degree. I had forty first cousins, twenty-eight on one side and twelve on the other, and exactly two of them, both superb athletes, had gone away to college—one in Maine to play football, and the other in Michigan to play baseball—but none of our relatives, and no one among the many people we knew in the city, had ever thought of living away at high school.

I liked Phillips Exeter best, had been offered a partial scholarship there, and wanted to enroll for ninth grade. That summer after eighth grade, my father sat with me in our enclosed, unwinterized back porch, and asked if I really wanted to go away to Exeter.

I said that I did.

"Well, you're not mature enough to live away from home."

"But Pa—"

He held up a hand. "I'll make a deal with you. You go to St. John's Prep as a day student for two years—it's only half an hour from here. I'll drive you up there every morning, and Ma can drive you home in the afternoon—and, for eleventh grade, if you still want to go to Exeter, and if you get in, and if we can afford it, I'll let you go."

And that's what happened.

At Exeter in those years scholarship students were required to hold part-time jobs on campus to help 're-pay' their awards, and all students were required to participate in sports in each of the school year's three seasons. I had no problem with the first idea and loved the second. In my first fall season, I ran JV cross-country, then played club ice hockey in winter, and JV baseball that spring. In my senior year I played club golf, then hockey again—my favorite; I was starting center of the intramural traveling All-Star team—and then tried out for and failed to make varsity baseball.

It was spring of senior year. The New Hampshire weather had finally turned warm, our heavy load of schoolwork was easing a bit as we moved toward the finish line. My closest friend, Chris Jenks, and I had both failed to be chosen for varsity baseball—he was a much better player, but a one-year senior, and seniors were at a disadvantage in the selection process because coaches wanted to cultivate their good players for several years—and so Chris and I decided we'd sign up for club golf and take things easy during our last months at Exeter. But when we walked up to the golf course, anticipating a jovial cruise to graduation, we learned that the golf roster was full, so Chris signed up for club baseball (and ended up leading the league in batting) and, for reasons I'm still not sure about, I decided on club rowing.

Let me take a step back. I mentioned above that

my connection to rowing had a mysterious aspect, and here's the best I can do by way of explanation. Once a week, as Director of Workmen's Compensation for the State of Massachusetts, a fancily-titled but low-paying job, my father was tasked with driving to various places in the state and inspecting the safety features of factories large enough to self-insure with the Commonwealth. Every once in a while, in summer and on school vacations, he'd take his oldest son along. Me. On one of those trips, headed for Western Massachusetts in springtime, we drove through Boston and along a raised highway that led to the Massachusetts Turnpike. Even now, that stretch of road offers a view down to a bend in the Charles River, which runs between Boston and Cambridge. As we were going along there, I glanced to my right and happened to see a crew shell, a team out practicing. I started yelling, "Pa! Pa! Look! Look at those boats!" My father had a temper, volcanic, if short of duration, and he yelled back: "Christ almighty! You almost made me drive off the road. Calm down!"

Why did I react that way? What could have been so spectacular about a couple of crew shells being rowed along a river hundreds of yards below us, that would make a working-class thirteen-year-old practically jump out of his seat with excitement? I'd never been anywhere near a crew shell. The races were never shown on TV. We didn't have any relatives who rowed and, to that point in my life, I hadn't even walked along the banks of the Charles River, not once. And there I was, yelling, "Look, Pa! Look!" so loudly that I'd nearly caused an accident.

When, after being shut out from another season of club golf, I decided to walk down to the Phillips Exeter boathouse and sign up for crew, I didn't have that moment with my father in mind. At least not in my conscious mind. At the boathouse, I first went through the customary week of training in a wide, flat-bottomed 'barge' that no amount of foolishness could tip over, then was chosen by Mr. Swift, a retired teacher and former varsity coach, for his 'Special Eight.' I was a senior. Word had it that Mr. Swift never chose seniors for his Special Eight. Like the coaches of other sports, crew coaches wanted to identify boys who seemed to have some aptitude, put them in the Special Eight, and then groom them for a position in one of the two top boats in their later years. But apparently Mr. Swift saw something in me, or the Hand of Fate was nudging him. He chose me for his Special Eight, and I took to rowing naturally and easily and enjoyed two months of practice under his kind tutelage.

That fall, on registration day at Boston University, varsity and freshmen crew coaches stood near the long lines of students signing up for classes, and recruited, or tried to recruit, the tallest students, because long legs and long arms are a decided advantage for a rower. They also recruited shorter students who didn't weigh very much, for the position of coxswain. At 5'11 1/2", and just north of 150 pounds, I was not among those they tapped on a shoulder and asked to go over to the boathouse for an introduction to the sport. But I went anyway. I endured another few weeks in the barge, shorter, lighter, but more experienced than all but a couple of the other guys, and then, when the freshman coach made his choice of the eight best rowers, I wasn't among them.

Technique and conditioning weren't the issue; in his eyes, what mattered was height and muscle mass—the rest could be taught. I was put into a four-man shell with three other undersized guys and a coxswain, and we were basically left on our own to ply the waters of the Charles while the coach rode along in his motorboat next to his eight best candidates in a different section of the river, upstream. Once in a while he'd swing by and give us a word of advice, but we all knew where we stood on the ladder, and we sensed that his advice was offered half-seriously, as if he really wanted to suggest we might be better off spending our afternoon hours in the student union, bowling tenpin and shooting pool.

Even so, I loved being out on the water, and was determined to find some outlet for my athletic interests. Crew was by far my best shot at making a college varsity team, so I kept going out in the four and splashing around, and, over the long winter season, worked out for two hours every day, even taking the subway daily, an hour and a half each way, to B.U., during our three-week Christmas vacation to lift weights, work on the ergometer, and sprint up five flights of stairs fifteen times in the rear stairwell of the Registrar's building. It's possible that at some subconscious level I knew the role crew would eventually play in my personal life; it's likely, I now believe, that I was driven by the same mysterious impulse that had caused me to become so excited at my first glimpse of a crew shell. It would be another year before that work would pay off and, despite my size, I'd be chosen for the first varsity boat, but that's not the point of this story.

From the Boston University boathouse, you can row east down the Charles to where it widens near M.I.T. and the Science Museum, or west into a narrower, curved section that leads past Harvard University. Most days in my sophomore year the varsity coach—a former Olympic gold medalist—took the two varsity boats west, where the water was calmer. But on this particular spring day, we headed east. The water was rougher there, the river wider and more exposed. The air was often colder. We did a variety of 'pieces', a minute, two minutes, ten minutes, depending on the coach's workout plan.

On this day, we'd broken up into fours and were doing a long piece, fifteen minutes or more, and were already tired from the hour of rowing we'd done, back and forth in the windy 'basin'. We were rowing along, only twenty-eight or thirty strokes a minute that early in the season, heaving for breath, trying to focus on timing and balance, on our technique, though our thighs were burning, arms and back tired, lungs aching, cold splashes from the other oars soaking our sweatshirts and faces. Anyone who's participated in a maximum-exertion sport—long-distance running, cross-country skiing, long-distance swimming, boxing—knows that, as the body is deprived of oxygen, the muscles begin to hurt. And as the muscles begin to hurt, the mind begins to counsel surrender in a loud voice. *What are you doing? Stop, please stop! This is crazy. You're causing yourself pain, and for what? What's the point?!*

And every other imaginable strategy the mind can think up to get you to go easy. For whatever reason, on that day I was keenly aware of this strategy. I can remember it even now. The thoughts were so convincing, so persuasive, so logical, and, like my teammates, I was in so much distress, physically, that the voice seemed particularly clear. I'd ignored that voice on other days: it's impossible to be an athlete and not learn to push your body beyond its comfort zone. But on that day I reached a new level of what I can only call *command* over those thoughts. I set them aside. I drove my body into new levels of pain and discomfort and felt like I'd won some kind of never-before-experienced victory over the interior voices.

As I said, that's a common experience for most athletes: baseball or basketball or soccer or tennis or hockey players also need to shut off the workings of the mind and let the body perform as it's been trained, even when the muscles are weary and the mind is offering all kinds of distraction. I'd pushed myself through those thoughts countless times in the past, sprinting up the fifteen flights of stairs, using the dreaded ergometer, running cross-country at Exeter, rowing crew.

On that day, though, something was different. Near the end of the long piece of rowing, I felt like my mind exploded into another dimension. Having set those thoughts so confidently aside, I leapt up into a realm that was nothing like anything I'd experienced. My mind was clear as a crystal, not empty, exactly, but clean, open. And that openness was accompanied by what I can only call ecstasy.

We finished the piece, cooled down with a few minutes of easier strokes, paddled the shell back to the dock, lifted it on the coxswain's commands, carried it into the boathouse and set it carefully on the rack there. We climbed the creaking old stairs to the locker room, stripped, showered, dressed in our street clothes again, and walked across the B.U. bridge back toward campus. Most of my crewmates were headed for the dormitory or cafeteria, but I was a day student and headed home. Every day after practice I crossed that bridge and, after a hasty snack, walked another half mile to the Green Line trolley stop to save a nickel on the fare, took the trolley beneath the city to Government Center, and waited on the lower-level platform there for the Blue Line train to Revere, where I'd catch a bus as far as Broadway then walk the last half mile home. On good days, when I made the connections quickly, the trip might take an hour and fifteen minutes. On bad days, two hours.

That day, from the crew shell to the locker room to the showers to the walk down Commonwealth Avenue, to the hour or more on trolleys and trains, I was enveloped in a state of something much more lasting and powerful than the typical endorphin rush physical exertion often brings. Nothing I'd ever experienced came close to that feeling, and nothing has come close to it in the ensuing fifty-one years. It was a kind of exultation. I floated along, exuberantly happy, but not in a laughing, smiling, outgoing way. It was all interior, as if my mind had hopped over the fence of the corral where it had been held captive for nineteen years and was cantering across a grassy meadow beneath a perfectly blue sky. No clouds, no fences, no one chasing me, no obligations, no worry, no plans, no fear of any kind. A *liberation,* it might be called.

The feeling lasted until I went to bed that night; it was gone when I woke up. But as I lay in my upstairs room in the darkness, looking at the light fixture above my bed, my parents and brothers asleep in other rooms, Elemosina came to me for the second time.

I won't keep repeating this, but I'm going to describe her visit here as a conversation, and it wasn't a conversation, not really, unless an exchange of mental energy can be called a conversation. There's simply no way to accurately tell you about her visits without using terms like 'voice,' 'woman,' and 'conversation'. And without giving her a name.

I sensed, again, her presence. It wasn't as if I could feel a ghost in the room. It wasn't eerie. In fact, though the visits were extremely rare and irregular, they always felt absolutely and perfectly natural to me, more natural, in fact, than anything else that happened in my life. Even after all this time and all these years spent thinking about those visits, I struggle to describe them in a perfectly truthful and accurate way. Maybe the best I can do is say that, when I sensed her presence, it was as if nothing else existed. Or as if I were completely separated from everything else, almost as if I'd been cast far out into space and there was a vast emptiness surrounding my spirit, my essence, and then this other *being* or *consciousness* appeared. It was as if we were two stars in a limitless sky. A sense of complete quiet, of the cessation of time. And then:

You don't seem too puzzled by what happened

today.

I tried to tell her that I didn't feel puzzled, but I couldn't find the word for what I did feel. *Puzzled* wasn't right. The feeling was new to me, unique. But, at the same time strangely familiar. Almost ordinary.

Which is exactly what death will feel like, she said, as if reading my thoughts.

I found that impossible to believe.

I tried to convey that to you last time, years ago, on the steps of the school on the day after your grandfather's death, do you remember? But you were so young, and you were surrounded by so much grief, and you'd had no experience of death in this lifetime, none at all. There was nothing wrong with your sorrow then, as I said. It was and is the appropriate response. But it's also something people feel because everyone else is feeling it. It is learned.

What happened to you today won't happen to you again for many years. It's a great gift. You've been introduced to another dimension of mind.

It felt like heaven, I wanted to say, and, again, it was as if she heard my thoughts.

Heaven is not a bad comparison. It was a glimpse of another dimension of consciousness, and even though you'll soon stop thinking about it, the memory of it has marked your awareness at a deep level. It's like cutting initials into a tree when the tree is young; they remain there as the tree grows. There's nothing you can do to repeat what happened today. It's a gift, not a reward. Different people receive the gift at different times and in different ways, some only just as they're dying, a final comfort, some women in the midst of the pain of giving birth, some who come close to death and survive, some in moments of ecstasy or battlefield terror, and some, like you, in what appear to be ordinary moments.

It's a gift, but hurting others, committing evil acts, continually wrapping your thoughts around the search for one pleasure or another—those things make it impossible to receive the gift again in the future. Heaven, the idea of going to heaven after leading a pure life, is only a metaphor for this natural law. The 'sinners'—to use an improper term, but one with which you're familiar—simply close themselves off from the possibility of receiving this gift in any form and to any degree. It's as if a beautiful symphony is being played all around them and they've chosen to stuff something into their ears. The symphony is there, always, for everyone; many people simply don't listen to it.

"So there's a state where you feel what I felt for eternity?" I managed.

That's too crude a description. The 'state' you imagine, while not bound by time, is not static. And it's also something you shouldn't think about or try to analyze. At some level, you will never forget this day, but the pleasures and demands of youth will push it to the back of your thoughts, to be remembered only much later. What's important is that you now know such states of mind, of being, exist. That fact will be unforgettable unless you live a life of purposely turning your back on it, which you won't do.

Lastly, in the beautiful, unimaginably intricate design that is creation, the activity you were engaged in today, the sport through which this gift came to you, ordinary as it seems, will play an essential role in your life. It will lead you to your life partner, and to places that have nothing at all to do with rowing on a river, or sporting competitions in general, but that will have great bearing on your spiritual self. Until that happens, you won't even remember this moment. The feeling will remain, as I said, at the back of your thoughts.

So what do I do then? What now?

That question, that thought-question, was answered only by Elemosina's disappearance. I was back in my bed again, on the second floor of the gray-shingled house on Essex Street in Revere, Massachusetts, five miles north of downtown Boston. There was no great sadness or frustration to her disappearance. Still wrapped in the strange joy, I felt nothing but the deepest confidence and contentment.

I went to sleep and, by the next morning, was already back in my 'normal' state of mind. My thoughts were taken up with schoolwork and dating and rowing and family issues. Elemosina was absolutely correct: I'd *almost* forget about what had happened that day. I wouldn't think about it, not even the next time we rowed by that spot on the river, or when I walked from the boathouse to the subway stop. My ordinary life went on. But at some level—a level that was inaccessible to me in my daily living—nothing would ever be the same. And, as she'd promised, crew would one day play a central role in my life, a role that would have nothing at all to do with sports. It would lead me to the woman who is your maternal grandmother.

The Third Visit
Stranger in a Strange Land

For some people, my dear grandchild—and maybe for you—travel is another passion, another teacher. When I was a boy our family didn't have money for exotic trips, or even not-so-exotic ones. The best my parents could afford was a couple of three-night vacations spaced years apart at a motel near Lake Winnipesaukee in New Hampshire, an exceedingly modest place owned by my father's friend, Bunny White, who kindly gave us a discount.

We lived a mile and a half from Revere Beach, however, which was Greater Boston's version of the much more famous Coney Island, and the three-mile beach, amusement rides, and games of chance there happily occupied my brothers and me most summers. But from an early age I longed to travel. I'd lie on a towel on the beach, watch the planes coming in to land at nearby Logan Airport—El Al, Aer Lingus, Swissair, Lufthansa, Al Italia, British Airways—and feel like the world was calling. After finishing graduate school (a Masters in Russian Language and Literature at Brown) the first thing I did was head off across country with a friend, and since then I've traveled almost compulsively: the former USSR, Scandinavia, Eastern and Western Europe, 49 U.S. States, Italy eighteen times, Jamaica, Puerto Rico, Guam, Micronesia, Canada, three months in Mexico.

Elemosina liked to tell me that seemingly ordinary events like choosing a major in college or taking a trip, aren't ordinary at all. Everything, she kept insisting, is connected. Everything. She assured me that the idea of coincidence is only a creation born of human ignorance and a deep, subconscious fear, and that everything on this Earth, every choice and event, no matter how apparently inconsequential, is part of an unimaginably intricate design. "The design has a purpose," she often said, though she refused to tell me what the purpose was.

For years I resisted her theory, clinging to the idea that events were at least partly random, and forces like luck played a major role in people's lives. But then, as the years passed and I was able to look back across longer periods and gain a clearer perspective, I came around to agreeing with her: there's no such thing as coincidence. I know others disagree, and I'm fine with that, but in my opinion everything that happens to us, good and bad, exultant and terrifying, is like the slow construction of the intricate cathedral that is a human soul. Every day, every word, every piece of suffering, every hour of pleasure, every thought, every relationship, every encounter, every night of sleep and every dream—it's all another block of stone or line of mortar in the cathedral. Some moments in our lives are grand and enormous—parts of the cathedral foundation, the walls, the roof. Others are tiny and seemingly insignificant—and those would be like the carving at the end of a wooden pew, or one colored piece of stained glass in a window. Taken together, they form the continually evolving human soul.

Here's an example: I speak Russian—thanks, or so I always believed, to an odd coincidence. In August, 1967, when I received a letter containing my list of ninth-grade courses at Saint John's Prep in Danvers, Massachusetts (where, as I mentioned earlier, my father had told me to spend my first two years of high school instead of going away to Exeter), RUSSIAN was listed as one of them. My parents and I thought it was a clerical error, or maybe a joke played by an admissions director with a sly sense of humor. Or that it was a coincidence, a fluke, my name drawn from a hat.

It would turn out to be anything but coincidence, and that one small turn in the map of my fate would evolve into a major highway running through my life from age fourteen well into my forties. With nine other freshmen I was placed in a classroom overseen by the Russian-born Mrs. Sloane, who was married to an American. Mrs. Sloane wore calf-length skirts and her abundant hay-colored air wound in a tall beehive on top of her head. She was a mixture of fierceness and tenderness, mostly encouraging but apt to lose her patience with our small, struggling, often irreverent group of teenage boys. (As you, yourself may know, teenaged boys, in the U.S. at least, have it rough, and sometimes make a lot of trouble for themselves and others.) One day, tired of our antics, Mrs. Sloane approached the desk of a particularly cheeky boy in the front row, scooped up his three textbooks, marched over to the second-floor window and threw them out.

While not quite deserving of that treatment, I was nevertheless a terrible Russian student. At night in my father's basement office in our house, I stared at the verb conjugations, trying to make sense of them. English had no such array, and the minuscule amount of French I'd taken in seventh and eighth grades had never included a study of grammar. In English we have "I talk" and "you talk" and only a small change for "he or she talks", right? In Russian, all kinds of strange things were happening at the end of verbs, and past-tense endings changed with the gender of the speaker. Those kinds of grammar intricacies, the new alphabet, and the twenty-four possible endings for an adjective depending on whether it modified a masculine, feminine, neuter, or plural noun and which case it belonged to (nominative, genitive, dative, accusative, instrumental, or prepositional)—all of it made me frustrated and sometimes depressed. Although my father spoke some Italian, he'd had no experience learning a language from a textbook; and my mother, brilliant woman that she was, had no ear at all for foreign languages. To complicate matters even further, I was used to being at the top of the class, used to all things academic coming easily, so I was—how foolish was this—

too proud to ask for help.

Somehow, I managed to squeak by in Mrs. Sloane's class—and then the following year in Mr. Sloane's—mainly on the basis of a half-decent accent and strong grades for reading aloud.

Junior year I transferred to Phillips Exeter, as per my dad's promise, and I continued my wrestling match with the Russian language, but it was as if I were in the wrong weight class, earning a D+ in my first term, and only gradually and with great effort and angst, rising to a B- by the time I graduated.

Russian Literature fascinated me from the first, however—Chekhov, Dostoevsky, Turgenev, Tolstoy, Leskov, Oblomov, Gogol—and so I kept picking myself up off the mat in the language classes all through high school, college, and graduate school, and, after earning a Bachelor's Degree and a Masters in Russian Language and Literature at Brown, I landed a job on a United States Information Agency traveling cultural exchange exhibit called "Photography USA", which would tour the Soviet Union in 1977. An enormous stroke of luck.

The USIA exhibit program was an attempt to penetrate the Cold War's almost impenetrable Iron Curtain. Some brilliant State Department diplomat had come up with a new strategy: we'd send exhibits on American life to the USSR, and the Soviets could send exhibits on Soviet life to the USA. In theory, a fair exchange. In practice, since the Soviet people weren't allowed to leave their country and were forbidden from receiving all but a thin trickle of heavily censored news from the West (they were allowed to see TV reports of police beating student anti-war demonstrators, homeless Americans sleeping in the street, or natural disasters on U.S. soil), there was, among them, an insatiable appetite for information from the rest of the world, especially from America. Our exhibits attracted 15,000 visitors a day, with waiting lines nearly a mile long. Later on, I would stop by one of the Soviet shows in Boston and see maybe fifty visitors there.

On Photography-USA, the first of what would be three exhibit tours for me, the last two with your grandmother, I served as one of the twenty-five Russian-speaking guides. Six hours a day, six days a week, we'd stand in front of a display of American camera equipment, or a wall covered with home snapshots, or a gallery of framed works by famous photographers like Ansel Adams and Alfred Stieglitz, or we'd translate for the visiting American professional in the portrait gallery, and we'd be surrounded by a knot of visitors. Leaning so close we could sometimes smell what they'd eaten for lunch, they'd fire questions at us, one after the next. How much does a loaf of bread cost in America? Why can't Black and White people sit at the same table in a restaurant? Why were your soldiers in Vietnam? Aren't you the son of a rich capitalist? Didn't your father get you this job? Tell the truth! What's your favorite musical group? How many square meters in your family's apartment?

It was excellent language practice, and, for all of us, a glimpse into a land so cut off from the rest of the world that it often felt like we were living on another planet. We stayed in Soviet hotels, ate in Soviet cafeterias, saw huge swaths of the country on our brief vacations, and were regularly invited to have meals at the homes of locals brave or naïve enough to take the risk of hosting us.

The exhibit showed for six weeks in each of three cities—Ufa, Novosibirsk, and Moscow—and, in each city, the guides and staff spent two weeks helping set up the 10,000-square-foot show, and ten days taking it down.

We scheduled the second city, Novosibirsk, for the heart of summer, because it was too cold there during most of the rest of the year. To my surprise, Central Siberia in June and July was blazing hot, and, thanks to the longitude, daylight lasted almost until midnight. One day, a young female visitor waited for the crowd around me to disperse and she asked me out on a date, suggesting we meet at the workers' cafeteria behind the ballet hall that evening. She was blond and pretty, and we'd been warned about KGB operatives trying to seduce us into giving away secrets. I didn't have any secrets to give away, and wouldn't have in any case, and once we'd spent a few minutes in the café I understood that Tatiana wasn't an agent, just a curious, bold young woman who'd chosen—by coincidence?—to ask me out, instead of asking out one of the other male guides.

Tanya and I started to meet regularly after my long day of work was finished, just walking around the city at first in the extended evening light and then, later, taking the commuter boat up the Ob River to one of the uninhabited islands there and having what she called a '*piknik.*' I'd bring a can of nuts and some bread, and she'd bring cheese and tomatoes, sometimes a piece of fruit and two bottles of the tasteless Soviet soda. We'd ride along the wide Ob to one of the islands, get off there, sometimes together with a few amateur fishermen or other young people out for an evening. We'd have our picnic and talk and kiss, but Tanya was eighteen, and things never went beyond that: talking and kissing, sometimes a swim.

On one of those excursions, she and I traveled to an island we hadn't seen before, and walked around to the quieter back side for our picnic. It was a good night for swimming, and we lingered longer than usual. It's possible that at one point we might have heard people calling from the pier on the other side, but we paid them no attention. When we finally decided to walk back to that side, catch the boat and head home, we realized it was close to midnight. Standing on the small pier in the riverine darkness, we began to understand, gradually and terribly, that we had missed the last boat back to the city.

In front of us was the mighty Ob, a mile wide at that point. On the far shore the lights of Novosibirsk. The invention of the cell phone was still decades in the future, and there were no phone booths, homes, or occupied buildings on the island, and, at that hour, not another soul. After we'd stood there for a few minutes with no sign of the commuter boat, Tanya started to cry. "My mother will be furious!" she sobbed. I was worried for her, of course, but mostly thinking about what would happen if I failed to show up on time to catch the bus to work the next morning. The exhibit director would have my room checked. Finding it empty, he'd summon the police. The police would call the American Embassy in Moscow. The director would worry about foul play, public embarrassment for the show, a black mark on his career. When I eventually got back to the hotel and told him what had happened, there would be a good chance I'd be sent home in disgrace.

Swimming across was out of the question. The width of the river, the current—no chance. We stood there on the pier in the starlit darkness, regretting our foolishness, and buried, each of us, in our own worries.

And then—by chance?—we heard the sound of oarlocks and quiet voices. *"Pomogitye!"* Tanya yelled out across the water. Help!

No answer.

We heard the knocking and splashing of oars again, a bit closer.

"*Rebyata! Pomogitye!*" Guys. Help us! "We missed the last boat. I have to get home to my mother!"

A voice from the darkness: "Sister, we can't. The boat is already too heavy."

"Brother, please, please! We missed the boat. Please take us across!"

For a stretch of half a minute we could hear only the oars in the oarlocks, and the small splashes, but there was no response. It seemed clear that we were going to be stranded there all night and face some very unpleasant consequences in the morning.

And then a small rowboat carrying two young men glided up next to the pier.

"Don't say a word!" Tanya told me in a harsh whisper, though, even without hearing my accented Russian, the two young men in the rowboat would certainly suspect I was a foreigner. I had a beard—which almost no Soviet young men wore then—and green-striped, white Adidas running shoes—the kind of treasure that was inaccessible to them. Hanging out with foreigners wasn't technically illegal, but, depending on the Party official at one's place of work, consorting with an American could endanger one's employment.

We climbed down into the boat, Tanya thanking the two young men profusely. I sat quietly in the stern, facing the rower; Tanya and the other passenger sat next to each other in the bow. We started off without introductions.

The current was strong and we were heading diagonally against it. After a minute or so, I realized that one of the oars wasn't an oar at all, but a rough-sawn two-by-four, one end narrowed into a handle. In the starlight I noticed that the man rowing bore an eerie resemblance to Robert Kennedy Sr. With the makeshift oar, the current, and the weight of four bodies, he was straining so hard that the veins in his neck and temples bulged and he grunted with each stroke.

I said nothing. Tanya and the other young man exchanged a couple of quiet sentences. I watched the Robert Kennedy lookalike row, making excruciatingly slow progress across the wide, dark Ob. We had no lights and I wondered what would happen if a cargo ship came barreling downstream. Mostly, though, I was at peace, grateful that we'd been rescued, enjoying the cool night air, the adventure, the feeling of being out on the water.

Fifteen or twenty minutes later we'd almost

reached the far shore. The current wasn't as strong there and the rower didn't have to strain as much. Another few minutes and the bow ground up on a gravelly strip of beach. We climbed out. I asked Tanya, quietly, if I should offer the rower some money, but she shook her head, no, not done, "such an American idea!" We helped the two young men push the boat up onto the sand. I risked two words, *"Bolshoye spasiba."* Many thanks. Tanya hugged each of them in turn. The two of us set off for the nearest bus stop, waited until her bus arrived, the last bus of the night, and said our goodbyes. I made my way across the city alone, heading for the Intourist Hotel and a few hours of sleep.

From my first minutes in the U.S.S.R., riding with my fellow American exhibit workers from Sheremetevo Airport into Red Square, I'd been surrounded by a feeling I find hard to describe now. It was March, 1977, the depths of the Cold War. We were in a place cut off from the rest of the world, a nation whose capital city featured wide, almost empty boulevards lined by rows of ugly, poorly-constructed apartment buildings, the only light coming from the few plain-looking cars that passed us (they rode with their parking lights, not their headlights on), a smattering of lit windows in the apartments, and neon signs over a few small stores. Those signs, spaced at half a mile, were generic: *Fruits and Vegetables. Bread and Rolls.* No names of owners, because the State owned them. No spark of individuality at all, anywhere.

All through our briefing at the American Embassy, all through the two months in Ufa, our first showing city in the rolling Ural hills, all through the breakfasts in the top-floor cafeteria there: horsemeat goulash, lumpy kefir, boiled hotdogs with peas; all through the conversations on the floor in the amazingly complicated but increasingly (to me) understandable Russian language, and then, when we finished up in that city, all through my five days on the Trans-Siberian railroad, traveling the empty territory from Khabarovsk near the Chinese border to Novosibirsk in the middle of Siberia with two co-workers—all those months we'd been enveloped in a great sense of secrecy, what Winston Churchill called "a mystery wrapped in a riddle wrapped in an enigma." Before traveling to Moscow, I'd been outside the United States only for three driving trips to Montreal, five hours north of Greater Boston, so every hour I spent in the Soviet Union was filled with the exciting sense that I'd been transported to an utterly alien dimension of life.

That night on the Ob felt like the perfect symbol for the mystery that had surrounded us for those months—the fear of trouble, the rescue, the immense darkness of the river, the lack of conversation or introduction, just the plain fact of the boat-owner's incredible generosity to people he didn't know and would never see again. Walking home through the sleeping city, surrounded by sights, sounds, and smells to which I'd become only partly accustomed, surrounded by—buried in—that feeling of Otherness, grateful to the center of my bones that Tanya and I hadn't been stranded out on the uninhabited island for the whole night, I had my third visit from Elemosina.

She began, as always, without prologue. *All the evil*

on Earth, she said, *has its roots in humans' inability to see beyond the surfaces of other human beings. Look at what just happened to you. Notice how Tatiana and the young man who helped you referred to each other as 'brother' and 'sister'. That can be seen merely as a cultural quirk, the way people in this country speak to each other. But it's actually an ancient form of address, an acknowledgement of kinships that the modern world—your world—has lost the ability to understand. Your world concentrates on the surfaces and uses them to divide. Nationality, ethnicity, skin color, facial features, age, gender, religion, sexual preference, politics, even the kinds of work people do and the amount of money they have—all these have their place, of course, and can be important, especially in the battle for fair treatment. But, for millennia, those surfaces have also been used as excuses for divisiveness, for the failure to look deeper.*

This is part of what you are to learn here, in these months, in this place that feels so alien to you. These people—Tatiana and the others, your good new worker friend Anatoly—are showing you a way to bridge what seemed, before you made this trip, an unbridgeable chasm between the people of two nations at odds with each other. Everything you'd heard about Soviets is in the process of being turned on its head by your personal experiences. I'm speaking of the people, not the government, which is an abomination to the human spirit. You can decide to see the people here as your enemies, or you can decide to see them as your brothers and sisters. In actual fact, you are all 99% alike. You have two lungs, a heart. Your systems—digestive, respiratory, circulatory—work in precisely the same way. And your emotional lives are equally similar: all of you want to love and be loved; all of you want to avoid pain and increase pleasure; you have worries, fears, hopes, dreams, and, allowing for cultural differences, those are all fundamentally the same.

As you go forward, you should remember this night. Rather than concentrating on the superficial differences you notice in other people, try to look into the pupils of their eyes—identical to your own pupils—and feel your way into their depths. Imagine their hearts beating in a rhythm similar to your own. In your daily life, of course, you can't fail to notice that someone is male or female, old or young, of one race or another. But try to shift your focus beyond those elements and, when you speak with another soul, concentrate on the sameness, the humanness, the spirit of that person. You believe you were given the Russian language by coincidence, but of course that isn't so. That 'coincidence' began your introduction to Russian Literature, known for its soulfulness, yes? Why is it known for that? Because the genius of the Russian authors you studied and still love lay precisely in their ability to write about the depths, not the surfaces, to create works that have lived already for more than a century because those stories have their roots in the emotional, psychological, and spiritual soil all humans share. The difficult language, the magnificent literature, your experiences here—highlighted by what happened to you tonight—are all part of your spiritual education. Others take different paths. Spiritual learning comes to them via scientific study, prayer and contemplation, love and devotion, or selfless service of one kind or another. All those paths can *lead you to where you eventually must go. Some people will live blindly, ignoring the lessons, living on the surfaces of things, but this job, this night, offers you an opportunity to look deeper, do you see?*

"I'm trying to," I said, and she made a sound like a happy laugh.

It's as if there are six billion rivers and streams on your planet (Eight billion as I write this; more, I'm sure, when you read it), spiritual rivers and streams. Each soul travels along one of them, often with company, sometimes alone. The moments they experience—moments of worry, fear, beauty, hope—while different, individually, are all linked to the water on which they travel, water that inevitably empties into a shared sea. Don't lose sight of that. Don't fall prey to the dividers, the ones who choose—out of ignorance or by conscious, willful decision—to focus on the surfaces.

Also, from now on, have faith that you shall be taken care of, which is the other lesson from this important night. You shall be taken care of. That doesn't mean every dream will come true, or that you'll be rescued from every difficulty. There will always be disappointment and pain, perhaps even terror and trauma. I'm not allowed to speak of those things. You will suffer, just as everyone on Earth suffers. But have faith that those moments, joyful and terrible, will ultimately lead you to the place you must go. Think of the moments of despair you and Tatiana felt on the pier, the worry, the imagined repercussions. They were like a miniature version of greater, existential troubles, of the worry-filled life. Sometimes you have to call out, reach out, ask for help. But, ultimately, be as positive as you can in those moments. Keep the faith, as the expression goes.

"Faith in what?" I asked aloud. "And where do the lessons lead?"

There was only silence. I crossed the last broad avenue and could see the faint lights of the boxy, bland, four-story hotel a block away, a hotel reserved for foreign visitors like me and my colleagues, and for members of the Soviet elite. I stopped there on the sidewalk for a moment and breathed, looking at the plain buildings, feeling the foreignness of the city, not tired in spite of the late hour and the night's excitement. I supposed Elemosina had said all she was going to say, because she never signed off with a 'good-bye for now' or anything like that; she just stopped 'speaking' to me.

But then, this: *Faith in the Ultimate of Ultimates,* she said. *The faith in which you were raised has carried you this far. Your own language, your own customs, foods, cultural specifics, religious practice—they have carried you to this point. Your task now is not necessarily to abandon them, only to open your mind to other ways of seeing the mystery that is a human incarnation. Believe, in your heart, even in the most difficult moments, even as you endure injury, sickness, and pain, even as you eventually approach death, that there is a grand purpose to your travels along the particular river that is your life. Instead of narrowing your focus, widen it. See the commonalities, in people, and in systems of belief—systems which are actually attempts to explain the Purpose. That purpose cannot be contained in words or thoughts, remember that. You can use your good analytical mind for many things, but not to answer the greatest questions. If you let it—and therein lies the key: if you let it—your mind and your behavior will be molded by every experience. What happened tonight is something you will never forget, but there will be countless other lessons, as if the Great Sculptor is cutting a block of marble, chip by chip, to form or expose or release your soul, your essence, which is brother and sister to every other essence in the universe. The same water, the same marble; choose how you wish to think of it.*

I stood still and waited, but heard nothing more from her. A militia car passed slowly by, the officers in their gray uniforms staring at me with a mix of curiosity and suspicion. I tried to see into them, beyond the uniforms. I made a casual friendly wave, human-to-human. They glared at me for a moment then turned their faces forward. I began to walk. At the glass door of the hotel, the uniformed man on duty at first refused to let me in. I tapped on the glass a second time, and stood there. He was shaking his head. The hour was late; he was there to protect the privacy of the privileged guests. Despite my beard and running shoes, I must have looked to him like an ordinary Soviet trying to pass for a foreigner, and ordinary Soviets weren't allowed into the hotel. I stood there. He glared at me. At last he opened the door a few inches and I wanted to say, "Look at my running shoes, listen to my accent," but what I said was, "Brother, I'm here with the American exhibition. I'm sorry it's so late." And he made a half-bow and swept his arm in toward the lobby like a welcoming butler from the years before the Revolution. I took the elevator to the fourth floor, the *dezhurnaya* on duty handed me my key without asking where I'd been. I went into my room, took off my clothes, and fell into a dreamless sleep.

The Fourth Visit
Trusting

Before I describe Elemosina's fourth visit, I want to tell you something you might already know: the start of true adulthood can be a daunting, disorienting time. If you're finished with college, or otherwise leaving your parents' home, or if, as I did in my early twenties, you've completed a temporary, eight-month job in another country, a job that paid well and provided housing and food, you'll be faced with decisions you never had to make when you were living in your old bedroom or dormitory room, when you were being fed at your family's dinner table, in a school cafeteria, or the restaurants of foreign hotels. If you choose not to attend college—as either your aunt or your mother did—then you'll be even younger when you face the question of what to do with your life, where to live, how to earn money.

It may be that, at 20 or 24 or 28, you still won't know what path to follow in life. If I were giving advice, I'd advise you only not to cling to a career purely and simply for financial security. Financial security is important, of course, but if that's your guiding principle, you might end up financially secure and otherwise miserable, spending five days of every week, and fifty weeks of every year, and the best years of your life, in a job you dislike, driven by the illusion of security ("illusion" because we never really know what will happen to us in the next second).

So, let me pass on to you what Elemosina told me: somehow it works out. In my mid-twenties I was confused, worried, comparing myself unfavorably and with a lot of envy to friends who seemed to have their whole lives planned out. They knew where they were going; they were already doing great things; I was adrift.

It worked out.

When the U.S.S.R. job ran its eight-month course, I returned to Washington for a week of debriefing and paperwork, and then, not knowing what else to do, went home to Revere. My parents were happy to have me there in the house on Essex Street, but it was clear that, after all I'd seen and been through overseas, I couldn't keep living with them. For two weeks I slept in the bed I'd slept in as a boy, in the large, second-floor room that looked out on what had been my grandparents' house, pondering, worrying, musing, wondering, figuring, trying to make sense of the past and chart a course for the future. The truth was, I had no idea what I wanted to do for a career, not consciously, at least. For a while, when the exhibit was showing in Moscow and we spent our last two months in the U.S.S.R. living and working there, eating at the U.S. Embassy cafeteria and going to parties at other embassies, I'd thought joining the Foreign Service might be the route for me. Several of the people I worked with on Photography-USA would take that route. Two would rise to the rank of ambassador; others would have long, successful, satisfying careers in cities across the Earth. But I'd seen how the Foreign Service families lived: moving every couple of years; followed and harassed by local security officials like KGB operatives; required, even within the freedoms allowed them, to espouse the official views of the State Department. It would be a life of travel and adventure, of honorable service, of helping to spread the ideals of democracy and fairness across the globe. But, stubborn and sometimes foolish guy that I was, some instinct counseled me against going that route. I don't know why.

What then? I wanted to do good in the world. I felt like I'd been given a wonderful life: loving family; great education; already, at age 24, an exotic overseas adventure of the kind most people would never know. But, given that past, what kind of future should I try to fashion?

Perusing the Help Wanted pages of the Boston papers, I came across an ad for a job working with challenged kids at a place called The Crotched Mountain School in New Hampshire. Growing up, I'd often seen ads for Crotched Mountain on the TV station my brothers and I liked to watch, and, during college, I'd done volunteer work with people who had physical and intellectual limitations.

So I called the Crotched Mountain School and said I wanted to come up for an interview. I told them I didn't have a car, and they said I'd need to get to the bus station in Manchester, New Hampshire. From there, I could take another bus that would drop me off within walking distance of Crotched Mountain.

I packed a small duffel, hugged my parents goodbye, rode the subway into Boston, and caught a bus for Manchester.

There are moments in a life that we remember with particular vividness. I can still recall one of those moments, still see myself standing at a ticket window in the Manchester bus station. "When does the next bus leave for Crotched Mountain?" I asked the woman behind the grill.

"There is no bus to Crotched Mountain," she said.

"But I called them yesterday. I'm applying for a job there. They told me to come here and catch the bus and it would let me off nearby."

"Well, there isn't any bus that goes there," the woman said bluntly. "Nowhere even close."

I went back and sat in the plastic chair of the waiting area. It's possible that, even then, I believed things happened for a reason. Maybe this was a sign: Crotched Mountain wasn't the place for me. Not wanting to turn around and head back home, I went to the window and asked the woman when the next bus left and where it was headed.

"Rutland," she said. "Rutland, Vermont. Leaves in thirty minutes."

"One ticket please."

"One way or round trip?"

"One way."

It was a three-hour ride to Rutland, the last hour along Route 4 in Vermont, a picturesque two-lane road that winds its way up the eastern slope of the Green Mountains and down the western side. Just as the bus was entering Rutland, which sits about half-way up the state of Vermont not far from the New York border, I saw a sign in front of a white clapboard cape: *Watermans' Guest House. Rooms.*

I walked back there from the bus station and ended up staying at the Watermans' for the better part of a month. The guesthouse was owned by Mr. and Mrs. Waterman, both named Fran. Decades later, talking to a man at the Rutland Golf Course, I'd learn that Mr. Waterman had been mayor of Rutland in his younger days, but, in the time I lived in one of their upstairs rooms, neither of them ever mentioned that. They were extraordinarily kind people and would sometimes let me share dinner with them, or treat myself to a couple of Mrs. Waterman's home-baked muffins.

Mr. Waterman was suffering from Parkinson's. On one of my first days there he told me he had to drive over to Lake Bomoseen to close up their summer house, would I mind helping him out? His hands shook so badly that he could barely control the car, but I rode there in the passenger seat, trying not to show any nervousness, trusting that things would work out, proud of myself for not making Mr. Waterman feel uncomfortable about his driving. I helped him put the storm windows onto their lakeside home, and we rode back without saying very much. Later that day, when I told them I needed to find a job, Mrs. Waterman suggested I talk to the people at the Killington Ski Area, some seventeen miles back up Route 4. "I don't have any way to get there, though," I said.

"Sure you do. Just stand out front here and stick out your thumb. You'll get a ride there and back, no problem."

The next morning I stood out beside Route 4 and one of the first cars stopped and drove me to Killington. The ski season was about to start, and they were hiring. I landed a job making sandwiches at the Peak Restaurant at the top of the mountain, at 4,000 feet. Every morning, as Mrs. Waterman had advised, I stood out on Route 4 and stuck out my thumb, and I was never late for work, not once. I had an abundant black beard, and was wearing a bulky parka and sweat pants over my jeans, and probably looked like I might cause someone trouble, but all kinds of people stopped to give me a ride. Mothers with small children in the car stopped. Grandparents stopped. Young kids just out of high school stopped. The kind people of Rutland would drive me to the intersection of the Base Road and the highway, and then it would be easy to go the rest of the way with other Killington workers. I'd catch a ride as far as the base lodge, then bundle up in blankets and ride the chairlift all the way to the Peak.

Some mornings it was so cold that when we rode the chairlift my co-workers and I would have to sit on one heavy wool blanket, wrap a second over our knees, and a drape a third around our necks and shoulders. If there was a wind, the chair would swing back and forth, side-to-side, bouncing over the stanchions in a way that made me uneasy. But it was a glorious ride, up to an altitude where the foliage was only stunted firs, frost-coated, and there were long-distance views across Vermont's high hills. Sometimes I'd reach the restaurant just as the sun was coming up above those hills in a blaze of orange and pink.

The work itself could be maddeningly boring: making overpriced microwave sandwiches for hungry skiers, filling the napkin holders in quiet hours, cleaning the kitchen. But I had money in the bank from the U.S.S.R. job and arranged to work only four days a week. On the other days, I pondered my future. I sat in the library listening to music on headphones, or took long, solitary walks through the city and along the snow-blanketed golf course, or hitchhiked to a nearby town for lunch—south to Clarendon, east to Ludlow, west to Poultney. Influenced by recent readings of Thomas Merton, I was trying to live in a semi-monastic way, getting up early, never letting myself nap, keeping busy, eschewing the drunken parties that were a regular feature of the other workers' nights. It was a lonely life. Sometimes I'd walk past the local bars and look through the windows just to see other human beings. But there was a new deep peace involved, too. I'd started meditating and had gotten interested in cross-country skiing. At the Watermans', I pored over two books that had been assigned for a writing class at Brown, years earlier: Martin Buber's masterpiece, *I and Thou,* and a book called *Saving the*

Appearances by the British mystic Owen Barfield. In college, I'd read only pieces of them—I was a lazy undergrad—but now I saw their value and read them slowly and carefully, making notes in the margins, often closing the books for a moment to consider a particular idea.

After a time, I moved out of the Watermans', to a cold, unfurnished apartment in the poor section of town called "The Gut." I bought a mattress and put it on the floor, bought some lumber, a hammer and saw and nails, and built myself a rickety kitchen table. I'd wake up at five-thirty, make myself a cup of tea and a bowl of oatmeal, dress in multiple layers, then walk fifteen minutes back up to the corner of Route 4 and Main Street and stick out my thumb. I developed a mantra, "God will abide" and believed, as Elemosina had told me, that everything would work out. I'd be taken care of. There would be difficulties, but I'd survive them. And, even if I didn't survive them, that, too, would have a purpose, would be leading me somewhere. I was stubborn and confused, but also, in a certain way, fearless.

On one of those work days we had to stay late at the restaurant. When the day was finally finished, we rode the chairlift down to the base lodge and my coworkers went their various ways, most of them to company housing along that access road. I caught a ride as far as Route 4, but it was so late that all the skiers and other workers had already driven off. I stood out there in the winter darkness and piercing cold, winds howling across the hilltops and through the valley. I was wearing my dark green parka and dark blue sweat pants and I wondered if anyone could even see me there on the shoulder of the highway, let alone stop to give me a lift. A few cars passed at long intervals. For once, no one stopped. I was starting to wonder if I should try to walk home, all seventeen miles, when a Vermont State Police cruiser pulled to a stop just beyond me. I wondered if I'd be chastised for standing out there so late, if I'd be seen as a suspicious character.

When I approached the car, the trooper asked me where I was going. "To Rutland. I just finished work."

"Hop in," he said.

He was young and red-headed and asked where I lived in Rutland.

"126 Robbins Street."

"I'll take you there."

We said almost nothing else. He drove me to my door and wished me a good night. I thanked him, dropped off my sack at the house, then walked back into town, had a bowl of soup for supper, and went home.

That piece of generosity will always stand as a symbol of the kindness I encountered in Rutland.

I'd started writing then, in my spare hours, and was working on a poem called "The Rutland Wind." I might still have a copy in the attic. I was sitting there in my drafty apartment, with a pad of lined paper and a blue Bic ballpoint, working on one of the lines of the poem, when I felt the familiar presence. Strangely this time, Elemosina didn't speak. I felt that she was about to, I definitely sensed her presence, and I waited, but there was only the usual silence of that empty apartment, one car going by in the street, nothing more.

I didn't have work on the following day, so I decided to carry my cross-country skis out to the golf course and get some exercise. A small river ran through the course. On that day, as I'd sometimes do, I stood beside the river and concentrated on the gurgling water and tried to quiet my mind. I thought of Elemosina's comment about all of us riding toward the ocean on our six billion individual streams. I thought about the water starting as a spring or runoff, high up in one of the nearby hills, trickling down in a crooked line then joining this cold stream. The stream would bubble along and eventually, I imagined, feed northwest into Lake Champlain, from there into the Hudson River, and the Hudson would travel in a broad stripe down between New York and Connecticut and end up in Long Island Sound and the Atlantic Ocean.

Basic geography, but for those few seconds when I managed to quiet my mind, that unstoppable movement of liquid atoms seemed magical to me, part of a larger, intricate design. Just as Elemosina had said.

The question that haunted me was: where do I fit into that design? At some level I was grateful that the job at Crotched Mountain hadn't worked out, that I had the freedom of seasonal work. I knew I was setting aside those months for a purpose, stepping out of the flow of American ambition to try to understand where I should start my voyage into the great ocean of work and societal contribution. But I had very little idea what kind of work I should be aiming for, and felt a fair amount of shame connected with that. I'd been given a great education. I'd worked hard at Russian, and had the amazing gift of the U.S.S.R. job. And what was I doing with that? Making sandwiches for skiers thirty hours a week. Listening to music. Walking around.

As I stood there on that cold Vermont morning, on the empty, snow-covered golf course, I sensed Elemosina again, and this time she spoke.

You are learning to trust, she said. *That's wonderful. And you are learning to clear your mind. Also wonderful. Those two skills will be of great benefit to you as you move on from here, but so far the trusting has been easy, hasn't it? Things have almost always gone as you wished them to go. Fine education, good friends, world travel, excellent health. Trusting, accepting, saying 'yes' is so much more difficult when you face challenges like the one you are about to face. I hope you can maintain this state of mind when difficulties arise.*

I worried about what she was saying, of course. Maybe I was even momentarily afraid. But I was suffering then from a state of mind many young people suffer from—if 'suffer' is the right word: I felt invulnerable. Healthy, strong, capable. I'd lived in the Soviet Union, after all. I'd rowed crew, one of the most arduous sports. I hitchhiked back and forth to work, seventeen miles each way, and, even standing out in the darkness on that freezing night, waiting for a ride, I hadn't been concerned for my well-being.

I waited for her to say more, but this fourth visit was a strange one, actually two visits, one soon after the other, and her first words to me, on the golf course, were only a kind of prologue.

That Sunday I hitched a ride west to Poultney, a handsome old Vermont town with white marble sidewalks and marble foundations beneath the older houses. I'd temporarily set aside my confusion about the future. My mind was clear and calm. I was immersed in the present, and the simplest things seemed magical—the leafless trees, the wood frame homes with their steep slate roofs, the thick coat of snow. I sat on a park bench someone had cleaned off and immediately my mind stepped into a different zone, a pure presence, thoughtless but not sleepy, aware. A new kind of joy, quiet and vibrant at the same time, seemed to light up my brain as if it were an illuminated room. Not too bright and not dark, not asleep but not moving. An entirely different species of happiness from anything I'd known. The feeling didn't last very long, and wasn't either as powerful or as lasting as the moment in the crew shell on the Charles River, but I felt that it was clearly pointing me toward something. Or preparing me for something. And, of course, I assumed that something would be positive.

A few days after that I was working at The Peak when the boss told us a delivery was coming up on the chairlift, and that one of my co-workers and I should take the freight sled over there—a few dozen steps—unload the food and bring it inside. Workers at the hut at the top of the lift had unloaded a dozen or so twenty-pound boxes of hamburger, and my coworker and I were charged with transferring them to the freight sled and carrying them into the Peak's kitchen. I lifted the first box and held it against my chest, took one step, and my feet went out from under me. I fell backwards and landed, upper-middle-back first, on the metal bar of the freight sled, with the heavy box held against my chest.

I lay there in intense pain, looking up at the sky. My co-worker asked if I was all right. I said "not really" and lay there, on the verge of passing out. After a few minutes, I was able to get up onto my hands and knees, and then get to my feet and, with some difficulty, make it back to the restaurant. I told my boss that I'd fallen and hurt my back. She told me to take the rest of the day off and make an appointment with the company doctor. She wrote down his name and phone number and I carried it with me, down the ski lift, and hitched a ride back to The Gut.

I lay flat for the rest of that day, took three ibuprofen, and saw the doctor a few days later. I told him what had happened. He examined my back and said, "Well, you probably just cut a muscle. No need for an X-ray."

I was twenty-four years old and had no experience with doctors trying to protect the company that sent them patients. After another day off, despite severe back pain and all kinds of spasms and ripples, I returned to my job at the Peak.

For years after that fall I had daily pain and sometimes debilitating spasms, and, whenever I could afford it, went to see chiropractors and massage therapists. One of those chiropractors took an X-ray—this was six or seven years after the fall—and when he'd pinned it up against the backlight he said, "So when did you break your back?"

"I never broke my back," I answered, thinking he'd mixed up my film with someone else's.

"Really? Come over and look at this X-ray. See this," he pointed to a vertebra with a thick white strip angling through it, and a mess of rib heads in an awful constellation nearby, not quite where they were supposed to be. "This is what a broken back looks like."

That was forty-five years ago. Since then I've had hundreds of back spasms, many of which sent me to bed for a few days, one of which sent me by ambulance to the local emergency room. I've spent probably $150,000 on various treatments not covered by insurance, and eventually had to stop doing some of the things—hockey, running, karate—that I loved. *One step,* I sometimes think. One step changed my life. But I know that many, many people have suffered much worse, and I know that, had I been a few inches farther from the sled when I fell, I would have hit my neck, not my upper back, and likely been paralyzed for life. So should I be bitter about that day or grateful for it?

Elemosina didn't visit me right away. She didn't visit me again, in fact, until many years later on a Labor Day weekend when I had such a terrible spasm that I couldn't lift myself off the kitchen floor and was taken to Cooley Dickinson Hospital in Northampton, Massachusetts, by ambulance. I have a high tolerance for pain, but this pain was of another dimension entirely, and when the ambulance went over a speed bump near the Emergency Room entrance, I screamed. I was examined, given a shot of morphine, and sent upstairs. The morphine took the pain away but made me nauseous. I had to be careful about moving, but I managed to reach up very slowly, pluck a paper cup from the table beside the bed, and vomit into it. I couldn't reach the call button. Two women were making an empty bed on the other side of the ward and I called to them for help, holding the cup carefully so I wouldn't spill it. "A nurse will be in soon," one of them called back.

"But I threw up into this cup and I can't really move. Can you take it?"

"The nurse will."

The nurse arrived in a few minutes, and when she told the doctors what had happened, they switched me from morphine to dilaudid. That medicine was injected into my upper thigh, and, after each dose I floated off into the most delicious sleep imaginable. I woke from that sleep in the small hours of the morning, not high exactly, but preternaturally calm. Except for quiet snoring from the nearby beds, a reflected light and the beeping of a machine in the hallway, and the sound of rubber-soled footsteps there, the whole ward was silent and dark. I managed to turn very slowly onto my back and lie as still as possible, just breathing, remembering the pain but not feeling it, trying not to think about what lay ahead. More surgery? Time in bed? Permanent damage?

And then I sensed Elemosina's presence. The feeling was familiar to me by that point, though it had been a long time since she'd visited. *I'm sorry you have to go through this,* was the first thing she said. *One of the aspects of the part of creation I inhabit is a dramatic intensification of the sense of compassion. It's not that I feel your pain, or your fear or worry; I do not. It's more that I can imagine it with an acuity that's impossible in the human realm.*

The other part of that, though, is a sense of the ubiquity of suffering. Buddha has been quoted as saying, "life is suffering." Of course, he didn't mean life is only *suffering, but, even in his human form, he was already in a realm somewhat like the place from which I speak to you, and from this place, it's impossible to ignore the vast amount of suffering on Earth. Not just the wars and torture, the murder and rape and starvation and grief, but suffering not brought on directly by other human beings: cancer, accidents, various horrible illnesses and the painful treatments for those illnesses. And that's not even taking into account the immense amount of non-physical suffering, which can be as great or greater—the loneliness, the heartbreak, the terror and confusion and depression.*

It's sad and peculiar to us in this realm that humans weep over death, when, in fact, death is a respite from the suffering you live with. Part of my work, part of our *work in this dimension, is to try and alleviate that suffering. We can't prevent it; we can only offer to those people who are open to other dimensions the opportunity to consider their lives from another perspective*

One thing you ought to keep in mind is the fact that you are not being singled out by some sadistic Creator. You suffered today. Your pain was quite intense. And you have suffered for years, as I predicted you would in that visit on the snowy golf course that morning in Vermont, do you remember? You will continue to suffer, in various ways, at certain times more than others. I can't go into specifics. You will, of course, reach a place where the suffering ends, but in the meantime I want you to remember that you haven't been singled out. Try, if you can, to imagine what is going on in this building at this hour. Yes, there are successful surgeries, recoveries, the alleviation of pain. There are glorious moments in the childbirth wing, great happiness there. There are people getting dressed and leaving even though they thought they would never leave. But in many of the rooms on this floor and others, there is deep misery. Try, if you can, to unite yourself with those people, with that suffering. It is not to be taken lightly. But see if, without adding to your discomfort, you can imagine your way into the lives and minds of those patients in the other rooms of this building. Try to feel connected to them, to feel as if you are enduring these miseries together, almost as one body. Not in a morbid, but in a compassionate way.

You can, as you've realized, look back on the accident that has led to this moment and feel an overwhelming bitterness. Why did you make that one careless step? Why did you happen to hit the bar of the freight sled instead of the snowbank? Why did your boss send you to that particular doctor, and why did he mislead you?

But I know you realize that you could also be grateful that you weren't paralyzed, that you haven't spent the past forty-five years in a wheelchair, being fed and cared for and living in an institutional setting. The back pain, awful as it has been, has led you into the practice of yoga, has enriched your contemplative life, and, most importantly, has made you into a person who feels compassion for the physical suffering of others. Be grateful for that, even now amid your discomfort and pain and fear of the future.

One thing you should know is that spirits new to this earthly realm, those who have not yet spent many lifetimes suffering, are locked inside their own feelings. It is impossible for them to reach their mind out toward others—which is what I'm asking you to do here in an advanced way. And so, in the extreme cases, those people can torture, they can rape, they can murder, they can torment and kill animals, or beat another human being to death, they can abuse others without being able to imagine what their victims are feeling. . .. without, in fact, even being able to imagine their victims as full sentient creatures like themselves.

Others, who have lived many lives and suffered in all of them, can step out of their own situation to some degree and feel compassion for their fellow beings. Love *is another word for that. Love is being able to put yourself in the place of another, and there are many degrees of that ability.*

You are not expected to enjoy this difficult time. You do not have to smile and laugh at pain and express sincere gratitude for it, as the great Masters might. Bu, you can learn to see it as an opportunity to increase your capacity for compassion, to move out beyond the self-imposed and entirely artificial limits of your own body and experiences in that body. There are countless variations of the ability to love, and lifetime by lifetime, experience by experience, hours of suffering and hours of joy, you will have the chance to learn to love more deeply.

Use this night, then. Use this difficult time here for that purpose.

And then she was gone.

*

I should mention here, as postscript to this section, that, on the day before I left Rutland, I walked back up to the Watermans' place and spent a little time with them, thanking them for their hospitality and kindness and saying good-bye. Something very strange happened on that visit—which had been unannounced—something that shows, I think, both the level of Mrs. Waterman's grace, and something else, some kind of mysterious connection we had, maybe, or maybe just the depth of her intuition. Before I left she handed me "a little gift for your travels," as she put it, a new copy of a large-format paperback book called *The Artist's Way*. I paged through it for a moment, wondering if she'd gone out and bought it specially for me—that seemed to be the case—and, if so, how she'd known I'd return to say good-bye. I looked up and thanked her. It was a sincere thank you, but a puzzled one as well. I didn't think of myself as an artist then, or even as having any particularly artistic tendencies.

Mrs. Waterman, one of those angels that appear in a person's life, was obviously far ahead of me.

The Fifth Visit
The Idea of Being Eaten

It's beautiful the way life works sometimes. As I was writing and rewriting this section—which is about what might be called a 'near-death experience', but is also very much about a young person trying to figure out his place in the world—I happened to have a conversation with your aunt or mother, who has been trying to figure out *her* place in the world. At the time of that conversation, she was 23, close to the age I was in this section, not long out of college, without having yet found a particular career path. (She has a Fulbright to Uruguay next year, however, so no one is worried.) Sitting at our kitchen table in the hills of Western Massachusetts, she and your grandmother and I explored that subject. We encouraged her, as I'll encourage you here, and as Elemosina often encouraged me, to have faith that things will work out as they're meant to work out. You should exert some effort, of course. It's your precious life, and you should certainly spend time pondering how you want to live it, where, with whom, and doing what, and then take the appropriate action. You should also be grateful that you have so much say over the matter: many people in the world have little choice in what they will do for work and where they'll settle.

This is a long section. I'd ask you to read it with all the above in mind—that things will work out, that you have to put in effort, that you're fortunate to have the choices you have. And also that, along the way, all kinds of things will happen to you, fascinating things, unexpected things, sometimes frightening things. And they will all lead you to where you are supposed to go.

*

Near the end of my time in Rutland, when the deep cold had eased (some nights there during the darkest weeks of winter the temperature dropped to minus thirty-five) and the ski season was drawing to a close, when my back pain had become more or less manageable and I was still wrestling, every hour it seemed, with the question of what to do with my life, I had a ride back to Rutland from a young man who told me, over the course of our half-hour conversation, that he'd been a volunteer in the Peace Corps. I don't remember how the subject came about, I remember only that the man—probably in his early thirties—told me he'd served for two years in Central America and that the experience had changed his life in a positive way.

Another moment that seemed coincidental.

Even when I was a young and curious boy, reading about the world, I understood how fortunate I was. I had never been hungry, homeless, or without medical care. For whatever reason, I was acutely aware of those who had much less, so the idea of becoming a Peace Corps volunteer, of giving two years of my life to ease others' suffering, struck a strong chord with me.

I went through the necessary steps: the application, the interview, the references, and after a wait of several months (I'd gone back home to live with my parents by that point, and was coaching crew, part-time, for ten dollars a day, at the Noble and Greenough School. More about that later.) Since I'd volunteered to work with blind people, I applied for a position working with the blind in Morocco. I didn't get it, and waited impatiently for a new assignment to appear.

And then, finally, I had a phone call from someone at the Peace Corps office in Washington. "There's an opening in Micronesia," the person on the other end of the line said. "On the outer atolls there." I told him I was interested and wanted to leave as soon as possible. There was a brief hesitation, and then, "I have to tell you that, along with Nepal, Micronesia has the highest dropout rate in the world for volunteers. The isolation, especially on the outer islands, gets to people."

I told the man that isolation didn't bother me, I was ready to go.

My parents threw me a backyard going-away party, and then there was a five-hour flight to Los Angeles, a day or two of meetings there, then another five-hour flight, to Honolulu. The other new Micronesia volunteers and I spent one night there—all I remember is staying at a cheap motel near the airport and walking along Waikiki Beach in the dark—and then boarded the plane again for a ten-hour flight to Guam. There, thirty or so other American volunteers and I stayed three to a room at a luxury resort frequented by Japanese honeymooners. My back seemed to have largely healed. I got up at six and, with three other volunteers, ran four miles before that heat of the day descended. A shower, breakfast (first time I ate seaweed), a morning of classroom instruction in subjects like soil chemistry and tropical diseases, and then, after lunch, more practical subjects: learning to pilot a motorboat, taking lifesaving and drownproofing classes, watching slide presentations about all the dangerous species that could be found in the tropical Pacific: the deadly Tiger shark, hammerheads, fire coral, lion fish, stonefish, moray eels.

We finished training and were flown to various Micronesian districts—The Marshalls, Ponape, Truk, Yap, Kosrae. I was in the Truk group (the name has been changed to Chuuk now, which better reflects how it sounds in the local language) and was sent to live with a family in the village of Sapuk, where I was scheduled to receive another month of language training before being sent to the outer islands.

Sapuk was not really a village, just a dozen or so tin-roofed houses on a jungle hillside. I had a small room to myself: concrete floor and concrete-block walls, louvered windows, a mosquito net, and a quarter-inch-thick woven pandanus mat for a bed. In the house's one other and much larger room, twenty-two people slept. Samurai and Miako were the names of the owners of the house. Their children, children's spouses, and only grandchild lived there, along with a troubled distant relative named Matteo, who spoke some English. From their house, it was a five-minute walk down a steep, slick path to the water, where a stone dock had been built by Trukese slave labor during the Japanese occupation. From that dock, it was an hourlong taxi ride in the back of a Toyota pickup to Moen, the island's only real city, a strip of tarred road and junky shops along the harbor where small fishing boats and the larger field trip ship docked.

Weekdays, I walked for the better part of an hour along a jungle path and had language lessons at Xavier High School, a building of thick stone walls and wooden doors that still bore the scars from a WWII strafing. Afternoons, I put on mask and snorkel and, very very slowly, learned to spearfish in the crystalline waters between the Japanese Dock and the reef.

That underwater world was a glorious living aquarium. Schools of silvery fish darted this way and that, sometimes completely enveloping me as I snorkeled along. There were enormous groupers gliding by, and slim, silvery barracudas angling this way and that. Morays in the coral. Black-tipped sharks in a feeding frenzy near the reef. I could see, underwater, for two hundred feet, and I loved paddling around there as much as the local children loved jumping off the end of the dock and making big splashes.

One of the other inhabitants of the house was a man named Antonio. About thirty years old, Antonio was married to Emma, Miako and Samurai's oldest daughter. Emma weighed over two hundred pounds—her heft being a sign of great beauty on the islands—and Antonio, at six feet, was a giant among the short islanders, built like an NFL running back, and as handsome as Emma was beautiful. They had a young son named Eine, four or five years old, who liked to run around naked with his naked pals. He and his friends would be out at sunrise, sprinting and laughing and screaming, a cacophonous island alarm clock that woke me every morning.

Like many of the islanders, Antonio had no paid work. He spent his days up in the hills, harvesting copra and gathering breadfruit, or out on the sea, fishing. He'd nod to me. We'd exchange a few words. But I felt with him—as I've felt with a handful of men in my life—an immediate connection, a mysteriously deep man-to-man acknowledgement and mutual respect. He seemed to sense my discomfort in that new world, my eagerness to be doing something of value, but we never had much of an extended conversation. He'd sometimes come and sit with me in my room when I ate—under Samurai's watchful eye—but even on those nights, he said little.

And then one day, when I was in the main room finishing a typical breakfast of salted fish (dried on the house's metal roof) and breadfruit, Miako said something to me that, despite my language training, I didn't completely understand. I asked her to repeat it, and she said, "Antonio wants to take you to his home island on Saturday. You can bring friends if you want."

I was surprised and flattered.

That trip, to Antonio's home island, would end up being one of the most memorable days in my seventy years on this planet.

Years later I was able to write something about that day. It's called "The Idea of Being Eaten" and I'll include it here. It's on the long side, and 'writerly', but it describes what I expect will be the greatest adventure of my life. . .and one of my most important visits from Elemosina, so I hope you find it entertaining.

*

The Idea of Being Eaten

We push off from the stone dock—built with Chuukese slave labor when the Japanese occupied these islands before and during World War II—and cruise slowly out toward the cleft in the innermost reef. Samurai's boat is a sixteen-foot wooden launch, partially covered by a sprayhood and propelled by two fifty-five-horsepower Johnson outboard engines. Besides Antonio—Samurai's only son-in-law—his four-year-old son, Eine, and my colleagues Bart and Duke, the cargo consists of five, ten-gallon canisters of gasoline, fishing lines, bait, handwoven pandanus mats, small gifts of food for Antonio's relatives, and two old floatation cushions. There are no life jackets aboard.

We pass through the cut in the reef and the bottom drops away. A moment earlier, the water running beneath the gunwale was a genial blue, color of the tiles on a Samarkand mosque, with fish drifting about as if gliding through liquified glass, and reeds waving this way and that at the base of the coral. Now, under a surface of teal green, that same water has gone blue-black, impenetrable, bottomless. It's a few degrees rougher here, too. A small chop slaps at the wooden hull with the bemused confidence of a polar bear toying with a seal cub it will eventually get around to devouring.

The day is magnificent—hot sunshine and a breath or two of breeze. A little way beyond the reef we're given a sense of the spaciousness of the Chuuk Lagoon, forty square miles of Pacific enclosed by the humpbacked protrusions of seven major islands and a few sandy specks. The sunlit faces the large islands turn to us are a bright rich green. Impossibly tall cumulus clouds float above them in even rows, like fat, flat-bottomed cotton soldiers passing in parade, throwing out and sucking in white knees and elbows, flipping elaborate tricks with their blue-tinted epaulettes and arms, for the benefit, not of us—we're inconsequential on this canvas—but of some parade-stand marshal of their own devising. Here and there amid their fluffy celebration I detect a sour note, something to be remembered only much later: a few of the passing recruits are dusted with dark gray or purple and, in places, a lagoon island—Fefan, Dubnon, Udot, or Tonn—lets its bright disguise slip, revealing a shoulder still cobalt blue in a last wisp of mist. Looking down the wide, flat, watery corridor formed by the island hillsides, it's impossible to deny the sense of some awesome, otherworldly presence, as if Samurai's *mota*, in crossing the first line of coral, has already borne us into a new dimension of possibility, some blue and jovial Oz.

As if to balance this ethereal beauty to starboard, decidedly unmystical plywood shacks and outhouses stand along the shore to port. A Toyota pickup races down the road there, spinning out a plume of dust. Banana plants droop in patches of sand that are littered with a debris of leaf and frond and coral stone. On that day, Chuuk island, my temporary home, looks particularly hot and stifling. I'm grateful to be getting away.

We move farther out from shore and settle in, the four full and one engaged gasoline containers taking up most of the bottom of the boat, heavy, blood-red, freckled with rust. Beneath the sprayhood, bottles of water, coconuts, mats, and spearfishing gear have been securely arranged so that the motorboat's bouncing and slapping won't knock them loose.

Antonio sits with the tiller held loosely inside his left elbow. Eine, a miniature replica of his dad, rests thin arms on his father's knee, absorbing the shock and bump of the waves as comfortably and naturally as a posting cowboy. Bred to the sea, able to swim shortly after they learn to walk, Micronesians are as comfortable on water as on land, perhaps more comfortable. Bart and Duke stand leaning forward against the sprayhood. The warm air flutters the cloth of their T-shirts so that they seem like two wind-whipped flags set at different heights on parallel poles.

I'm sitting midway between the back edge of the spray hood and the tiller, not far from Eine and Antonio, letting my fingers dangle in the water, watching our village of Sapuk as it's replaced by the the village of Tunnuk, and then, after a stretch of jungle, by the much larger town of Moen. In a short while, the brownish mouth of the harbor appears. Dozens of small boats are tied up there, bobbing like white toys in the brightness, their captains—in from the lagoon islands to sell or buy—walking barefoot along the wooden docks or standing together in poses of businesslike amicability. The field-trip ship is in port, white also but dwarfing the other vessels. Duke and I, both headed for assignments on the outer atolls, study it. He turns and asks when I'm scheduled to head out for my job organizing the ancient island laws and putting them to paper.

"First week of September."

"Who knows when it will really be?" he says.

Antonio holds our course north and slightly west. Moen's tar streets and square, dusty storefronts gradually fade. The lagoon islands stand well behind us now, their shoulders, cheekbones, and foreheads fallen into the sea, leaving afloat only the dark green tops of their pointed, rumpled caps. Fifteen minutes farther along we approach and then pass through the cut in the larger reef that surrounds the island of Chuuk and the greater lagoon.

These are the waters we will cruise in for the rest of the way to Antonio's place of birth (which is labeled Pis-Losap on the map, but pronounced "Peace NO-sahp" in the L-less Lagoon dialect in which I am called Ronan instead of Roland, and which gives us the English cognates of *nuv*, and *nadies*.) Here, the water stands hundreds of feet deep and is the playground of whales, marlin, and some of the largest sharks in the world, and it knocks our little boat up and around and side-to-side with an impertinent hand that, though still playful, is noticeably less gentle that it was inside the reef.

Behind us, one after the next, the summits of the lesser lagoon islands disappear. Chuuk, rising and then falling as if fighting a battle to stay afloat, loses it, and sinks from view as well. For another fifteen or twenty minutes, two very small uninhabited islands—ten acres each of sand and shrubbery with a few coconut palms glinting slivers of sunlight—seem to float along with us to starboard. Then they, too, fall away, and there is only the great expanse of sky, the great expanse of sea, and a rocking wooden vessel, significant as a fingernail clipping in a pond, ferrying five souls northward.

"How do you know your heading?" I ask Antonio in my still imperfect Chuukese.

"I just know, Ronan. I look at the small islands we passed just now, and from them I know."

"Do you ever make this trip at night?"

"*Ewer,*" he says. Sure.

"And how do you navigate then? By the stars?"

A nod.

"What if it's cloudy?"

"*Mi na,*" he says. By the waves.

"How, by the waves? What do you mean?"

"I can tell by the way the waves hit the side of the boat which direction I'm going."

Antonio says this in the most matter-of-fact tone, and I believe him. I have seen him lift the 200-pound Johnson engine to one shoulder and carry it up the steep slick path from the dock in his bare feet. I've seen him comfort a weeping child, fashion a harpoon, repair an engine, cook breadfruit, fix a broken flashlight, dive and coast along the bottom as effortlessly as a ray. So the idea of him piloting his father-in-law's irreplaceable motorboat across fifteen miles of unmarked water on an overcast night, and finding, by virtue of *the way the waves feel,* a flat, unlit island two hundred yards wide, is actually believable.

At six feet tall, Antonio is a giant among his people. Built like an NFL cornerback, as calm under pressure, prudent, fearless, dignified, interiorly still—he's exactly the kind of person you want to have around in a situation where lives are at stake. Which, as things will turn out on this mischievously sunny, apparently harmless day, is a lucky thing.

We bait three handlines with live, silvery fish the size of plump bananas and toss them into our wake. In Chuuk, there are no fishing rods: the islanders prefer to hold the line in their hands and, because of this, the leathery palms of old men are crisscrossed with long, thin scars.

Antonio ties the lines to the support bar of the sprayhood, then rigs up a length of black rubber tubing, about a foot long, in such a way that it will absorb a strike without snapping the line or tearing the wooden support from its place. Wise move this, as some of the edible fish cruising in the water below us weigh more than a thousand pounds. Some of the sharks weigh two thousand.

For an hour then we fall silent. As instructed, I hold my fingertips against the nearest line, like a Chinese physician reading the pulses, but there are no nibbles. Bart and Duke stand in the spray, a fine salt filigree building up on the lenses of their sunglasses. Eine moves from his father's knee over to the gunwale, then to my knee, then back again. He doesn't fidget or complain. Antonio changes position once, to shift the fuel lines when the first of our five tanks runs dry. Other than that, we are quiet and steady in the passenger half of our small wooden craft. There is the constant drone of the engines, the quick, asymmetrical slap of wave against bow, the equatorial sun beating down upon us—its brutal force muted here by the moving air, and by the occasional tepid shower thrown over us by a cresting wave. Beneath and beyond these surface distractions one senses something larger—the long, regular ocean swells, pulse of the planet. And beneath and beyond them, something larger still, some merciless and proper mystery that rocks and swings just on the far edge of the details of daily life.

As if standing in for these details, a smudge appears on the horizon ahead. It looks, at first, like a drifting cloud of smoke, but how could there be smoke out here? Antonio stands, stares at it a moment, then tells us to pull in the handlines as quickly as we can. He closes the throttle while we do this—twenty-seconds—then opens it full and the boat leans flat and forward like a thoroughbred in the stretch.

It takes us ten minutes to close on the cloud of smoke, half that time for the cloud to metamorphose into an enormous flock of seabirds. The birds are seagull-sized but trimmer, quicker, colored like chess pieces, all white and all black, and making their way rapidly west to east in a frenzied dance of looping ascents and straight kamikaze dives. Beneath them roils a purplish patch of sea. The birds are shrieking, diving, splashing; the school of fish that draws them is surging east, too near the surface for its own good. Lines still aboard, we race after them as fast as we can go, the prow of the boat jumping from the crest of one small wave to the next. For a few moments it's impossible not to feel joined to the wildness of the world, untamed, unprotected, speeding across the universe like a god among gods chasing gods. For that time—three minutes, five minutes—the pure dance of the present bursts up through the veil of fear and plan and calculation with which it is ordinarily covered (the system we call 'civilization' is so expert at covering it) and reveals to us its unveiled face. A war whoop, molecule of joy, forms in my chest and bursts free. The birds do not notice us, the fish do not notice us. They play on, dance of life and death, not the slightest part human. And yet, some frail thread links us. This animal excitement runs like a narcotic in the blood for a few minutes, until prey and predator speed away and fade to nothing in the east, too fast for us to follow.

*

Some of that exhilaration stays with us during the rest of the ride to Pis-Losap, a kind of afterglow, gift from the absolute present—which has now, so quickly, become fossilized in the past. "In wilderness is the preservation of the world," Thoreau wrote. Fossilized, too, that once-fresh sentiment is stamped on calendars and notecards, but the seabirds have given it fresh meaning for me. The music of things, a jazz riff of death and ecstasy, has sounded in my ear. As we move along now in its echo, flying fish break the surface and coast eerily by, bizarre, impossible creatures, holding themselves airborne for fifty yards, then flapping their side fins at the last and dropping suddenly back into the sea, more words from the Wordless.

After we've been in the little boat for close to three hours, Pis-Losap shows on the horizon, a low dark strip, rising into view and then disappearing again with the swelling and subsiding of the sea beneath us. Gradually, as we draw nearer, the island attains a shimmering, consistent form. Soon we can make out individual palm crowns, and then, lifting into view beneath them, a patch of beach the color of pear flesh. Flashes of bottom appear through curtains of brown reeds, and in another moment we're gliding across the marvelous gas-flame blue of shallow tropical seawater.

At first glance, Pis-Losap seems deserted. A few scraps of paper slosh in the shallows, where waves break gently in a flotsam of twigs and suds. Pieces of driftwood, not yet bleached, lay about in haphazard patterns on shore. Bart, Duke, and I jump overboard into warm surf. Antonio cocks the engines back to protect the propellers; we grind the hull into wet sand and drag it to safe anchorage on the beach.

Bearing gifts, Antonio and Eine go in search of their people. Bart sets off to survey the island on foot. Duke and I spit into our masks, rub a thin film of saliva on the inside of the glass to keep it from fogging, take up our spears and surgical-tubing slingshots, and wade in.

With a single exception, the snorkeling on Pis-Losap proves uneventful. There is no reef on this section of the island, no coral hive of life, only a bare sandy bottom, a few shivering plants reaching toward the light, and the occasional finger-sized *puna* floating lazily along, too small to grace a frying pan.

The single exception is a sea snake. On Guam, preparing to live in the Chuuk District of Micronesia and help bring some order to the ancient, unwritten laws, I'd been told with absolute assurance that sea snakes do not inhabit these waters. This error seems somehow appropriate. Places have a certain spiritual scent, and, so far, the scent of Pis-Losap is a dry, neutered one. It seems a forsaken place, the back lot of Eden, a spiritless territory avoided by birds, eschewed by fish, inhabited only by a hundred souls with the karmic bad fortune to have been born neither on one of the beautiful lagoon islands nor on the wilder outer atolls where Duke and I will soon be posted. And so it seems somehow correct to come upon a snake in these waters, where it is said not to exist—as if the rules made by the rest of creation cannot apply in this bland, aquatic suburbia.

Five feet long, thick as a child's wrist, banded in various browns not unlike the deadly coral snakes of my home territory, the sea snake wriggles through the blue a few feet below us. Duke, brave or crazy, makes a shallow dive, takes a shot with his spear, misses. The snake swirls on, exploring, uncaptured. Which, as it turns out, is our good fortune. Years later, telling the story of this day to a diver friend, I learn a bit about

Aipysurus eydoxii.

"Deadly poisonous," the friend says. "Did you know that?"

The first impression offered by Antonio's home island is soon confirmed. Duke and I are summoned to lunch, and we follow Eine along a crooked sandy path that penetrates the interior of the island. A few poor-looking houses stand in a clearing there—rusting tin roofs and stained plywood walls, one concrete-block schoolhouse built as a refuge for islanders during the frequent typhoons. Dogs, raised for their meat, slink in the shadows, children chase after hens, who lift up their tailfeathers and hurry into the bushes, clucking, annoyed. A handful of adults sit around, leaning against tree trunks and sucking at fish bones. We sit with them and are fed—plain fried fish, a little breadfruit, coconut milk. There are no introductions, only a few puffs of conversation sent out into the stifling air. How did such a place produce a man like Antonio?

I've heard stories of what it's like to be on these islands when a typhoon strikes. The summit of Pis-Losap stands less than ten feet above the level of the sea. In the time before concrete houses, people would sometimes lash themselves to palm or breadfruit trees in order to keep from being washed away. Nowadays safety measures are less extreme: on every inhabited island there is at least one building made entirely of concrete. In the strongest storms, the island's whole population crowds into this 'typhoon house', with two-hundred-mile-an-hour winds screaming outside the walls, and trees being torn up by their roots and carried away. The sea level rises. Sometimes the people inside the concrete house end up standing knee-deep in brine for a day or more. Once, on one of the atolls in the Hall group, fifty-miles north of Pis-Losap, a woman gave birth in those circumstances. Her baby, a young child now, bears a name that marks the event: Taifun. That is the island to which I will be sent.

Baked in Pis-Losap's noontime heat, wondering if the exotic promise of life in the outer islands will always reduce itself only to this—burning sand and noisy inactivity—I allow myself an uncharitable thought: at least, when the big storms come, the place must have some sense of excitement to it, some life.

Worse than uncharitable.

The sea-gods will exact an appropriate penance.

We finish our meal and sit in patches of shade in the stifling air of midday, watching the children scamper and screech and the dogs chew hungrily on fish skeletons at the clearing's edge.

Soon, Antonio stands, Eine parts reluctantly from his cousins, and we follow the path back to our small vessel. Antonio's family has given him a bowl of uncooked rice and some fabric for the relations on the big island. We stow these gifts and our fishing gear, push the boat off the little beach, and clamber aboard. A man who looks to be Antonio's brother stands in the water beside us, one hand on the gunwale, as if to hold us back. He's peering at the sky, apparently discerning some pattern there that's invisible to the rest of us. He and Antonio glance at each other, exchange a word. Then the brother pushes us off, Antonio lowers the propellers, clicks the engines into place, yanks once on the starting cord—muscles rippling—and in a puff of smoke and a bubble of churned up Pacific, we are on our way home.

At sea the air is ten degrees cooler and we quickly leave the lethargy of Pis-Losap behind. I take my place with my compatriots at the sprayhood, and we exchange a few words about the visit, about our future assignments. Eine stares over the side, looking for fish, but the handlines remain curled and stashed against a gunwale. Antonio sits surrounded by gas canisters, holding with one hand the metal steering bar that turns both motors in tandem. For the first half hour or so, the sea exhibits almost the same disposition we rode through in the morning; there's a slightly fresher breeze now, and a bit more spray—welcome enough—kicks up into our faces and chests. The sun still beats down jauntily, though there are more clouds. Perhaps we're in for an afternoon shower.

And then, forty-five minutes into the return voyage, as if a lever has been moved in some control room beyond our vision, we are abruptly traveling across a different sea and beneath a different sky. The change is dramatic in its suddenness, not in its degree. We have merely crossed the boundary between partly sunny and mostly cloudy, between the ordinary disturbance of the ocean surface and something not quite so ordinary. I can't explain why, but this new mood doesn't quite feel like the approach of the regular afternoon shower. Then again, I've never been this far out at sea during the regular afternoon shower. I have, until a few hours ago, never been this far out at sea at all.

"Getting rougher," Bart calls edgily.

I look back at Antonio to see what he makes of it. He sends me a big smile.

We continue along at a good clip. When the third canister of fuel runs dry, I help Antonio rearrange them so that the full ones are nearer, the empties off to the side. He lets his son clip the fuel line into place, lets him hold the rudder, tiny hand and tiny arm a smaller shadow of the father's. Three tanks used now, two in reserve—seems right for this stage in the voyage.

There is no land to be seen. With the thickening of the clouds, much of the color has bled out of the day, turning the cloth of the ocean into a wrinkled gray shirt, dusted with dirty white along the tops of the larger wrinkles. Now and again, making a heroic effort, the sun shoulders the cloud cover aside and produces an effect not unlike that of a yellowish searchlight being shone through the curtains of a dim room. For half a minute, for a minute, the day as it was is given back to us. The ocean brightens, seems to grow calmer. Drops of brine sparkle on the skin of Eine's brown arms, and small short-lived rainbows form in the spray. But soon the clouds muscle in again. The mood of the sea worsens in a wink. I put my sunglasses in my pocket and look over my shoulder a second time: Antonio is still smiling.

For a while we go on this way, riding a salty limbo between the traveler's natural optimism and the thickening gray reality above us. A bit too soon for my taste, Antonio engages the fourth tank. Eine holds close to his dad's knee—a four-year-old with the self-possession of an adult. Bart, Duke, and I take turns standing at the sprayhood and sitting on the slick wooden slat. For a time we float suspended beyond the rim of the wheel of the lagoon reef and its green mountainous hub, following an invisible line in the mind of our captain. Gray, breezy, petulant, the weather now seems poised between the jubilant brightness of the morning and something else, something we can feel in the cooled, trembling air, but uncertainly.

Another few minutes and the sun disappears, taking the uncertainty with it. A gust of wind plucks at the waves, the sky presses down, a smattering of hard raindrops pelts the sprayhood roof.

"This is interesting," Bart says.

"It's all right. Antonio's still smiling. When he stops smiling is when you worry."

But a small seabird of worry has found the boat and flutters along beside it: I search in vain for the atolls we passed on the way out, then look ahead, toward the place where the lagoon islands ought to appear, the horizon there marked only by thick purple clouds moving in a heavy, counterclockwise twirl. There are noticeable troughs now; our fragile craft bumps down into them, climbs in stuttering fashion, kicking sideways like a skittish colt.

It begins to rain, a steady, windblown *wani,* nice and cool against the skin. I can feel twinges of fear in Bart's posture, but so far the voyage is only made sweeter by the tossing of the sea—the way a few minutes of light turbulence can draw the monotony out of a long jet flight.

The wind stiffens. Behind the occasional gust there is now a strong steady breath. After a few minutes, the great mass of the sea responds to this change, or, at least, the topmost layer of the great mass of the sea responds. You can feel the weight of all that water more clearly now, glovetaps of a boxer with some link between shoe and mitt. Whitecaps snarl around us, the boat lurches, kicks, slips into and out of the irregular troughs, all its surfaces slick with rain and seawater. In the eastern distance—"eastern" here being an exercise in optimistic speculation—the charcoal gray of the sky bleeds down in thick, slanted bands, and at that place both sky and sea seem electrified. From here, that pocket of silent agitation appears almost benign, but you can imagine what's going on. I wonder if Antonio and his brother saw—or sensed—this in the formation of the clouds above Pis-Losap when they stood there gazing aloft.

Another minute and it becomes easier to imagine what's going on in the distance. I want to ask Antonio how he keeps his heading—not by the sun surely, not by these unpredictable waves, no compass or sextant on board, no map, no radar, not another vessel in view. But the wind and rain make conversation impossible. By now, in any case, it's clear enough that Micronesians can no more dissect and explain their mastery of the sea than an accomplished carpenter can provide a dissertation on the art of driving nails—the different hammer grips and strokes, the way an experienced eye takes in the grain and tension of the wood, angle and thickness of the nail, touch of the hammer's head. Antonio just knows where he's going, that's all, the way

Eine will someday just know it.

Ahead and to starboard the mottled flank of an enormous fish—shark perhaps—breaks the broken surface for an instant, then disappears. Five miles or so straight in front of us the ragged horizon is adorned with something too solid and dark to be a cloud. Then it, too, disappears, another mirage. Appears again.

"*Funu,*" Antonio shouts into the wind when I turn. Land. Not specified.

"*Funu,*" I say to Bart and Duke. "Land ho."

The wind grows stronger. A rolling, spitting rogue wave lifts and holds us, pushes us back and sideways, drops us without tenderness into its following trough. Rain falls hard for two minutes, then stops. I grab the plastic coffee can from the shifting cargo beneath the sprayhood and bail out the water that has collected around Eine's ankles. For a second, I take hold of his arm and squeeze playfully and he smiles, like his father, but tightens his grip on his father's knee.

We seem to be traveling as much in the vertical plane as in the horizontal and, after another quarter of an hour, the bit of land is not much closer.

The wind has been turned up two notches. There's no stillness to the sea now, not even the smallest element of consistency to the boat's dance. Bart has gone silent. Duke has put on his rain slicker. Eine huddles closer against his father, who smiles, still, every time I turn to look.

Smile or no, it has become abundantly clear that we're not passing through any ordinary afternoon shower. The tops of the nearest two lagoon islands have come into view, but we're moving toward them at a pace calculated to bring us safely ashore in about a week's time. Fifteen minutes later another inch of the tallest island—Tonn, it should be, if we are where we think we are—has risen from the sea. The boat dives hard into the troughs then points its nose up and climbs, crests, cuts through a white crown of surf, dives hard again. The rain begins anew. For the first time since leaving Boston, two months ago, my body remembers what cold feels like.

Crest after foamy crest, trough by trough, we make our wet way toward a point a few degrees to the left of the summit of the nearest island. The sky squeezes lower, beheading the three green hills in our range of vision. Every bit of clothing on our bodies is soaked through, water sloshes back and forth in the boat, the cargo knocks and jiggles, dribbles out around our feet. Antonio switches the line to the last tank of gasoline.

A sentry of very rough water guards the cut in Moen's reef. Rising and falling, skidding sideways, shuddering, its twin propellers lifting free of the water several times and screaming like tormented animals, the boat passes safely through this rough patch, through the cut, and into shallower water. The bottom is only a hundred feet below us now instead of thousands. But when we turn due south, instead of being calmer, the sea is rougher, running directly against the prevailing wind. Duke climbs over the sprayhood and wraps the prow rope around himself, riding the waves like a cowboy and leveling the posture of the boat. The snake-shooter. Five-feet, five inches of fearless Minnesota.

I look back at Antonio. No smile.

I think, for a moment, that he might head for Moen harbor—our home dock is still five miles or so to the south—but he does not. A seaman's pride, perhaps, in the presence of landlubbers. Or, more likely, a disinclination to turn the boat crosswise to the heavy seas. Instead, we move southeast with the shoreline, a hundred yards out from, and parallel to, the innermost reef, making steady but excruciatingly slow progress.

The rain has stopped again, but it barely matters: at the base and crest of every wave we're drenched by buckets of spray. Eine begins to cry. Hours and hours of a brave, thirty-year-old's stoicism, now he's four again. His face is contorted in grief, his fists are clenched. In his own language of tight muscle and tears, he's pronouncing the same *No!* to the source of the wind that all of us speak in our thoughts. I crouch and wrap my arm around him, let him shriek into one ear while the wind shrieks into the other. I look at the inner reef and try to imagine making the hundred-yard swim, with my pathetically inefficient crawl stroke and unbuoyant legs, in this water, holding a child. I wonder where sharks go in a storm.

The next thing that happens is that the engines give out. A quick sputter, then stillness. No longer driven forward against the wind, the boat swings around quite naturally, exposing its low open stern to the advancing surf. The top halves of two waves break over the engines and come aboard. Antonio is on his feet, tearing at the starting cord. The powerful muscles of his arm and neck flexing, every speck of concentration focused on the blue-banded motors, as if he's thrashing them, beseeching them, willing them back from the dead. It occurs to me that we may have run out of gas. Antonio rips at the cord again. Another dozen or so gallons of seawater wash into the boat. Again, he tears at the starting cord; the engines splutter and cough. Another try. Nothing. Another try and the engines come alive. He wheels us around. I throw the rice over the side and begin to bail with the big bowl, but we're calf-deep in seawater now, floundering. Antonio is shouting.

"Ron!" I hear, and the rest is rapid-fire Chuukese, windblown, lost to me. I shake my head.

"Home?" he yells. "*Imach*?" and gestures into the huge oncoming waves, their crests seeming taller now because we're so heavy with water. "Or over the reef?" He turns and points ninety-degrees right.

I don't stop to wonder why he's consulting me. I don't take into account the cost of his father-in-law's boat or the impossibility of the family ever replacing it. I hesitate for all of one second before pointing toward the reef. Antonio doesn't hesitate at all.

Once he turns us toward the reef, toward the calamity of roiling white that marks the border between safety and peril, we're broadside to the breaking sea, a flank exposed. The boat rocks like a runaway car in a demented amusement ride. The sky spins, the wind howls and whips and flings waves against us as if we're the advance guard of some heathen invasion and must, at all costs, be prevented from taking a beachhead. And yet there is something utterly impersonal about this fury, completely free of vengeance, entirely correct. We're the ones who make it personal. Only from the infinitesimally small outcropping on which we've set our telescope does our own pain and death appear as apocalypse. All we need to do to shed our terror is to step away from the eyepiece of that narrow lens and see the universe as it must see itself. The difference between Bart, frozen at the sprayhood, and Duke, still riding the prow, is nothing but a few degrees difference in this perspective.

The boat sinks lower, seems to be losing its will to stay afloat.

Seventy yards to the reef now. Duke climbs back and joins us.

I hold Eine in my arms like a younger, more frightened version of myself. If the boat capsizes, we'll have to swim for our lives through the shark-filled nightmare between us and shallow water. I have a clear sense of the veil of my taken-for-granted existence being lifted, a glimpse of the passage into death, and all I have to do to slip free of the fear is to abandon my perspective...and decades of being afraid of water.

Somehow, then, through some bestowal of grace, I'm able to do that. It's as if I jettison an enormous cargo of self-concern and will my attention into the wild heart of the moment. I'm alert to a degree I have never been in my life, surrounded by wailing demons, but not terrified. Fifty yards to the white fury. Keeping hold of Eine, I duckwalk to the port side, hoping to act as a ballast in this crosswind, but the boat's rocking barely eases.

Forty yards. Thirty yards.

Ten yards from the reef, Antonio dials back on the throttle. The water crashing around us is pure white,

Samurai's *mota* heaving and dropping like a Styrofoam cup in a destroyer wake. We float in an odd, shuddering standoff with the reef, not quite touching. Antonio holds us there, working the rudder left and right to keep us pointed straight in, gauging the movement of the rolling white mounds to windward, waiting, looking for the moment when he can play the one card left in his hand. It is not an ace. Timing the heft of the ocean perfectly, he waits until a shoulder of sea moves under us, then guns the engines. We fly over the coral berm on a three-inch cushion of froth and into the relative calm of a small, empty bay lined with whipping palm trees.

Antonio cuts the engines. He leaps overboard, I leap overboard. Duke is in the water, too, holding the prowline like the lead of a terrified horse. Set to the task of bailing, Bart calms immediately. Antonio and I are side by side, chest deep in sea, bailing, and comforting Eine. When the boy is settled and the boat relieved of most of its water weight, we turn it back to the reef, climb step by careful step, waist-deep in ocean, up the uneven mound of coral, and walk forward that way, pushing the precious boat along the spine of the reef, with the wind-whipped bay to our immediate right, and to our left, all hell, broken loose.

No one makes a sound, not even Eine. For the better part of an hour we go along like that, stumbling and slipping in the wind and rough surf, stepping off neck-deep into coral pockets we can't see, climbing back up, all the while struggling to keep the boat pointed toward Sapuk and to prevent it from blowing back out into the chaos of deeper water.

It begins to rain again, hard. Nobody cares. The water sloshing and slapping at our waists is warm; we shiver in it. Most of the light is gone by the time we come around a point and see, through the driving rain, a blurry, beautiful chip of shore that bears some keen resemblance to the Japanese Dock.

Another little way and we're walking downhill, water rising to our chests. We climb aboard, Antonio gets the motors started one more time, and with the last of the gasoline, ferries us home.

As we approach the dock in the rain and gale force winds, I see a plump figure working its way out along the slippery stones. Her husband and only child at sea in a storm, hours overdue, Emma has been waiting who knows how long in the flimsy shelter of who knows what patch of trees. Another moment and she's standing directly above us, wet dress plastered to her hips, thighs, and breasts, the wind whipping her hair out straight behind her, her gaze fixed on Eine's frightened face. As we nose up to the stones, she bends to take hold of the gunwale and says something to Antonio, several quick sentences of which I catch only a single word: *taifun*.

We manage to get the boat tied securely in a sheltered spot, and carry the outboards up to the little toolshed in the pelting rain. The wind shrieks and moans in the trees and rattles the gutters out front, through which rainwater pours, filling and then overfilling the barrel we drink from. Traversing the path to the outhouse is like wading through a shallow swamp, and the hillside back there is alive with thrashing new streams and a hail of green coconuts.

Duke and Bart stop with us long enough to drink a cup of instant coffee, then duck away through the storm to their own families, their own suppers, their own sweatshirt pillowcases stuffed with dry clothes. The house's plywood windows are hooked tight in the closed position, the main room is almost dark. Antonio, Eine, and I towel off, change into dry shirts and pants, and sit on the floor of my room with Miako, Emma, Samurai, and Matteo. Rain beats on the metal roof and courses down the blue-tinted windows. We shiver in the shadows thrown by the kerosene lamp, sip coffee, pay close attention to the periodic reports brought by Ekwa, a neighbor with a short-wave radio and a passion for drama. The typhoon is called Ennen he tells us. Ennen has turned east unexpectedly from Yap. Ennen (Elaine, but they can't pronounce Elaine) is moving our way.

And then, in subsequent reports, Ennen might be changing course again, north, toward Guam.

Ennen is turning back toward us.

No one knows where Ennen is going.

Other than Ekwa's bulletins, delivered every twenty minutes or so, there isn't much conversation in the room, not much in the way of dramatic retelling of the events of that day. Antonio is quieter even than his usual quiet self, embarrassed perhaps at having gotten us into such a fix, or afraid Samurai will find out that, two hours earlier, his irreplaceable *mota* had been driven over a reef. Or maybe he's just relieved to be home, with his feet on the floor, his knees raised, and Eine wrapped in a woolen blanket between them.

An hour later than our usual bedtime, with gusts still slamming against the house and Ennen's path still uncertain (it would eventually turn east and make landfall in China, 1,000 miles away) we bid each other sweet dreams and retire. Whatever might happen in the coming hours, we're safe behind these concrete walls, dry and safe, on solid ground.

I have, for some reason, packed a pair of long johns for my trip to the tropics. I pull them on over my legs, with socks and a sweater, and fall asleep to the rhythm of the wind: dry, warm, the floor moving under me.

I sleep soundly, waking once to a steady light rain, and again, hours later, to sunlight seeping through the trees.

The house is empty. I shoo flies off the rice, breadfruit, and slices of copra Miako has left on a table in the main room, eat every bit, and set off for Xavier High School and language classes. Palm fronds, shards of banana leaf, and baseball-sized green coconuts lie everywhere along the puddled path, as if some Messiah passed through here on a donkey the day before, triumphant, and this is the evidence that remains.

Classes that day are an exercise in anticlimax. Bart and Duke and I sit near each other at lunch, talk a bit about the trip, but don't feel inclined to entertain anyone with tales of our adventure. We're immersed in it still, trying to find the place where it fits into our otherwise safe and predictable lives. When classes are over, I go outside alone, sit on the stone wall at the edge of school property, and gaze down for a long time at the sparking ocean—calm now, and completely benign. This sunny world has become a sweet pretense hung like a curtain over a doorway. I've had a look behind that curtain, and what I saw there was hard-edged and vivid and merciless, but not terrifying. In a certain way, that other reality, stripped bare of the bright comfortable vestments of the wealthy world, is exactly what I came to Micronesia to see. I have seen it, and now, for the first time, I have an overwhelming urge to go home.

After a while I leave the wall and the expansive view and start down the grassy slope in the direction of Sapuk. On the road that runs along the edge of campus I come upon Antonio, who's climbing down from the hills with a partly filled copra sack over one shoulder.

"I am glad to see Ron on this day," he says in greeting.

I tell him I am glad to see him, as well.

"I was worried you would die yesterday. I was worried you would die, and on all the islands the people would say it was Antonio who had let the American guest die in the sea."

"You thought we'd drown?"

"Oh no, Ron," he says, as if the idea of drowning, even the idea of an American guest drowning, stands, for someone who grew up playing in the sea from toddlerhood, outside the realm of realistic possibility. "Oh no, Ron," he says again, "I thought we would be eaten."

So, my dear grandchild, as you can imagine, that day is deeply etched into my memory. I've often wondered if Antonio ever thinks about it. Probably not. Probably, if he's still alive (most Micronesian men die in their early sixties) he lives immersed in the present. But I do wonder sometimes if, when one of the typhoons that frequently batter the Central Pacific, tearing across the vast stretch of small islands, shakes the trees in his village, he remembers the moment when he turned to me and asked whether to cross the reef or continue on up the shore. His little boy was in the boat, their only child at that time. In terms of its preciousness, the boat itself would be the equivalent of the house of an American family, though uninsured. I was younger, a foreigner, someone with nothing like his understanding of the sea. And yet he looked at me, pointed, and shouted over the roar of the wind and waves, "Home? Or over the reef?" I wonder why I didn't hesitate, didn't shout the question back at him, let him make the decision. I'll never see him again, I'm sure of that, never have the chance to ask if he remembers. But I'm guessing that, once in a while, he does.

The adventure shook me, brought everything into question, including why I was thousands of miles away from home doing very little to help anyone. I remember, a day later, leaving the last language class and sitting alone on that same part of the stone wall not far from Xavier High School, a place with a view of the lagoon—so much quieter on that day. I remember it because it was there that Elemosina came to me for the fifth time.

You were such a fearful child, was the way she began. *You were afraid of water, afraid of fighting, afraid of firecrackers, afraid of the rougher kids, afraid of being embarrassed on the baseball field. You're still somewhat afraid of flying, aren't you? And of ocean swimming? Yesterday was the closest you've ever come to death, and the fact that you were able to focus your mind, look directly into that fear, and set it aside, was a major advance for you and something you will remember until you face the actual moment of your death.*

And then she surprised me by saying, *Congratulations!*

For what, I wondered. Congratulations for what?

The experience in the crew shell on the river in Boston, along with your meditation practice, have started to give you the sense that, as I reminded you earlier, you are not your body. There is some other, non-physical aspect of your divine spirit, and what happened to you in those terrifying moments in Samurai's boat was that you were able to at least partly focus on that other aspect of yourself. It also helped that you decided to concentrate on Eine, on easing his terror, not on your own fear and survival. I'm sure Antonio saw and appreciated that.

Just as importantly, you were also able to feel compassion for your friend who was panicking. Compassion, not pity, not criticism or mockery. Another major 'advance', though I use that word guardedly. You saw yourself in him, perhaps your former *self, and in feeling no superiority to him, so little judgment, you were, of course, feeling that way toward yourself. This is one of the great secrets of human existence: In simple terms, in order to love others, you must love yourself. In order to respect others, you must respect yourself. In order to feel compassion for others, you must feel compassion for the parts of yourself that are less than admirable.*

Your time in Vermont was of crucial importance, the start of your contemplative practice. Don't abandon it. That practice will wear away at your fears the way water wears away at stone, and perhaps you will end up one fine day becoming the kind of warrior who walks through the Earth without any fear at all, confident that he—or she—can face any difficulty.

In those few minutes in Antonio's boat you were able to see the line between what we call life and what we call death. You saw how thin that line is, how artificial. I mean 'artificial' not in the sense that the line doesn't exist. It does exist. Death is real, and it can be a great challenge for many people, and contain great terror for some. The ones who are least terrified are those who have died many times, shed their human body many times. The ones who are most terrified are those who believe they are their body. Naturally, if you believe you are your body, and if you believe the world revolves around you and your physical existence, then death must be traumatic. The end of you. The end of everything.

Death is, of course, a change, and should not be taken lightly. But what you saw yesterday is that there is a part of you that does not change, a part that simply skips over that line between this life and the next phase of existence. There is a part of your spirit, your essence, that is deathless, and you can learn to reside there, to remain there for stretches of seconds or minutes. The Great Ones can remain there always, even while they are on Earth.

The loss of your father's father was such a blow to you, as we've discussed, but from now forward, though there will be other losses and sometimes great sadness associated with them, they will never be surprising, and you will never feel that those spirits have ceased to exist, only that they are temporarily separated from you, that you cannot grasp them with your ordinary senses.

Little by little, if you persist, you will gain a deeper and deeper understanding of the actual nature of reality. You may have heard the phrase, from another great teacher, "Seek, and ye shall find. Knock, and the door shall be opened to you." You will have, at first, only a glimpse of a light that seems to be in another room, and then you will have more and more clarity of vision, more glimpses, and then, eventually, entry into that room.

Yesterday, by the way, you were in the company of a great spirit, as you surely understand, though perhaps subconsciously. Antonio is not an ordinary man, and the fact that he invited you on that trip was not accidental. He sees in you the potential to gain the kind of perspective that he lives inside of continually. He is one of the world's great sages in disguise, which is part of why he says so little. At this level of existence, his understanding simply cannot be conveyed in ordinary language. Sadly, you will have no further connection with him in this life, but that is as it should be. He has helped bring you to this moment. He has served his karmic purpose with you for now, and you have responded in a way that justifies his faith in you, that makes me happy, and that should make you happy, also.

I was pleased with her words, of course, by the 'congratulations!' especially, but they also deepened my confusion in a certain way. She seemed to know the future, and I was left only to worry about it. Elemosina departed as she always did, without warning or any kind of formality. I would stay in Sapuk for another few weeks, have one more grand adventure with Antonio, hunting turtles near the reef in the light of a full moon, and then leave for the outer islands. There, on my tiny atoll sixty sea miles to the north, I would be assaulted by a variety of tropical infections and a bad case of intestinal worms. To my great disappointment, I would discover that the job I'd come to do did not exist. I was of no help to anyone, except, one day, to a young man who cut his leg to the bone with a machete, out there, beyond the reach of any but the most elemental medical care. I had to tell the person who treated him to remove the tourniquet his father had tied around his thigh, and she did that only skeptically, reluctantly, then sewed up the gaping, oozing wound from the bone out.

The young man did not lose his leg, and found me on the island weeks later and thanked me. But there was no other work for me there, nothing but sickness and the most profound boredom. I spent the mornings snorkeling in the lagoon with my spear and surgical tubing, trying to catch something for lunch, and the afternoons sitting in the shade to avoid the brutal heat and humidity, making the fifteen-minute circumambulation of the island two and three times, waiting for my box of books to arrive (they, and a letter from my father, would turn out to be lost on route, though your grandmother—not even a girlfriend then—sent me a small box with cookies, music on tape, and a lock of her beautiful chestnut hair). At night the air cooled and my concrete block of a house was habitable again. The men from my part of the island would sit with me in a circle on the floor, drink instant coffee, and tell stories, then call the little girls in so they could add their soprano voices to beautiful acapella melodies they all sang.

But those blessed moments weren't enough to assuage the boredom, to make my struggles there seem worthwhile. I'd volunteered to help people and instead I felt like I was wasting my life.

The field trip ship stopped by the atoll once every two months. The second time it docked in the lagoon, I packed up my things and climbed on board. I sailed into the District Center and officially left the Peace Corps, much to my own shame and disappointment. It wasn't the illness; it was the frustration of doing nothing all day, helping no one. As with so much of what happened to me, I would understand the purpose of my time there only years later. *We see the reasons in retrospect,* Elemosina told me, and that has turned out to be true. But the shame of quitting stayed with me for years after I returned home, and touches me even now from time to time, though more lightly.

Before I left the islands for good, while I was staying at the Peace Corps office in Moen, waiting for my flight home, I bought a twenty-pound sack of rice for the family in Sapuk, and a big sack of oranges. I caught a pickup-taxi and rode back to Samurai and Miako's house to say my good-byes. When I told them I was going home, Miako, in a gesture of remarkable kindness and generosity (given the fact that twenty-two people already lived in her house), offered to let me sleep there, with the family, as part of the family, but I declined. I'd hoped to see Antonio and say good-bye to him, but, again, Elemosina was correct: I would never see him again. He was up in the jungle working. I asked the family to give him my best, to say good-bye for me, and I took the taxi back to Moen Town and, next day, caught the thirty-hour flight back to Boston.

The Sixth Visit
Love and Work

I'm going backwards in time here just for a bit.

I have to admit that, at the time of her visits, I believed only about half of what Elemosina was telling me. In retrospect, I see how foolish that was. I'm even a little embarrassed about it now. But I'm trying to be as honest as I can here, and the truth is that some of the things she said were so far out of the realm of the familiar for a person like me, so distant from the kingdom of the believable, that I swept them away into the corners of my waking mind. Only later, in some cases many years later, would I look through those dusty piles and discover the gems sparkling there.

She had told me, as you might remember from an earlier chapter, that rowing would be an important part of my life in ways that had nothing to do with oars and shells and water. I'll backtrack just a bit here and show how true that turned out to be.

Between the time I stopped working at the Vermont ski area and the day I left for the Peace Corps, I had some time to fill, two months. Shortly before the end of the ski season, I had a call from a friend and former B.U. crew teammate of mine who had heard about an opening for a part-time crew coaching job at the Noble and Greenough School in the Boston suburbs. He wondered if I'd be interested.

I took that phone call—as I took most everything in those years—as a sign from the Universe.

I moved back with my parents, started the coaching job, and realized immediately how foolish I'd been to accept it. Foolish in the practical sense: The job paid ten dollars a day, and it's not easy to go from one side of Boston to the other. It took me and hour and a half of riding on bus and subway to get within walking distance of the Noble and Greenough campus—then another mile on foot. I'd coach for two hours and have the long ride home in front of me. Often, I'd break up that part of the trip by wandering around downtown Boston, going to a movie, having a pizza. But, basically, I was using up a whole day for ten dollars. Even so, something that happened while I was working there would lead to my meeting, or re-meeting, your grandmother—another example of what now seems to me a pre-ordained pattern.

In spite of the inconvenience, there were some good parts to the coaching job. I liked being out on the water again, and liked the kids I coached. And the long commute had the advantage of giving me a lot of time to think about what I really wanted to do with my life, after I came home from what I expected would be two years in the Peace Corps. There were inklings now and again, whispered words about a writing career, the artistic life, but I immediately swept those thoughts over into another corner. Despite my fine education, I was, at heart, a working-class kid. I knew that my parents had made real sacrifices to send me to Exeter (where I had a half scholarship) and Brown (where my family paid the full load with a little help from my summer earnings. While tuitions in those days were a fraction of what they are now, so were salaries. Colleges were much less well endowed and much less generous with scholarship money, and the income level that warranted help was much, much lower than it is now.) Even if I'd had a shadowy inkling that I might want to write for a living, that career seemed next to impossible. I did not personally know anyone who made a living writing books, and I understood that the odds against doing so were astronomical. Besides, how could I tell my parents that, after all their loan and tuition payments, I was going to enter a career field with next to no possibility of financial security?

On one of my last days of work at Nobles and Greenough (My mother had let me use her car that day, since it was a Saturday and she didn't need to drive to the junior high school where she taught), I refereed a small, end-of-the-season regatta, riding along in my motorboat, watching carefully to make sure the start was fair and that none of the shells drifted out of its lane and interfered with a competitor. After the final race, I tied up the motorboat at the dock, said my good-byes to the other coaches and the kids, and made my way to the parking lot. I was just unlocking the driver's side door of my mother's four-year-old, five-speed, yellow Mercury Capri, when I heard two couples having a conversation a few cars farther along the row. They were talking about heading down to Providence for that day's Brown-Harvard crew race. Thinking I would save them a trip, I called over, "No, the races at Brown are in the morning."

That was true. Or had been true during my racing days on the Seekonk.

But one of the women called back. "Not today. Something about the tides. The races start in an hour."

Nothing particular was calling me back to Revere on that day. Noble and Greenough is southwest of Boston, and Providence is due south, so it would be only about a thirty-minute trip to my alma mater. On impulse, by chance, by coincidence, I decided to go.

I parked near the Brown boathouse—such a familiar place—and climbed up onto the flat roof viewing area to watch the finish of the races. Maybe because I was done with coaching and completely free, I was in a garrulous mood that day and remember making conversation with various groups of students there. I don't remember who won the races—Harvard, probably; they were next to unbeatable in those years—but I vividly remember leaving the viewing area and starting down the wooden steps. Near the bottom, I spotted a young woman climbing in the other direction. Her face was familiar. "Hey, Mandy," I said. "How are you?"

Mandy Stearns was three years younger, so we'd known each other only very slightly at Brown. We'd had overlapping circles of friends (she'd come to the boathouse that day to watch some of the rowers she knew) and had sat together at the large refectory tables a handful of times when I'd been a senior.

We fell into a long conversation. I told her I was waiting to go into the Peace Corps. She told me she was about to graduate, and thinking of taking a job teaching Spanish at the Emma Willard School in Troy, New York, the private high school from which she'd graduated. I gave her my number and asked her to call if she ever came up to Boston.

A month went by. I was at loose ends, waiting for the Peace Corps to call and tell me where in the world I would be sent. As mentioned in an earlier chapter, that call finally came: I was headed for Micronesia.

Early in the morning, ten days before I was scheduled to leave, the phone rang. I was still in bed. I heard voices down in the kitchen and, after a few minutes, my mother came upstairs and told me that my Uncle Pat, who lived next door, had collapsed and died at work. I was still wrestling with that news when the phone rang again. I answered this time. It was Mandy Stearns, coming to Boston for the day, did I want to try to get together?

I went across the yard to sit with my Aunt Philly for awhile. By then, other relatives had arrived, many of them bringing food, and I knew there would be three nights of wakes at the local funeral home, then the Mass at St. Anthony's, burial at Woodlawn Cemetery, and a gathering of all the relatives and close friends at the house next door, where I'd grown up. So I kissed and hugged my aunt and, after lunch, took the subway into Boston, met Mandy in the Back Bay and we saw the Burt Reynolds movie, The Dead. It wasn't out of any disrespect for Uncle Pat. By then, thanks in part to Elemosina and to the deaths of all four of my grandparents, I'd come to see death in a somewhat different light: still a sad occasion, but not the end of the existence of the spirit I'd loved.

I don't recall what we thought of the movie. Afterwards we walked over to the new Christian Science Church building that had an infinity fountain and a huge map of the world. Mandy walked me back to the Auditorium subway stop and there, at the top of the steps, we had the first of what would be tens or perhaps hundreds of thousands of kisses.

After my uncle's funeral and burial, Mandy and I had a wildly adventurous week. We traveled up to Rutland to see my friend Gerard, who'd taken over my apartment in The Gut. We stayed at a hotel in Exeter, New Hampshire, spent time at Forty Steps Beach in Nahant, and she came to the backyard party my parents threw for me before I left for Micronesia. I flew off to the islands and, instead of taking the teaching job at Emma Willard, Mandy found an apartment in Boston and a job there waitressing at a fancy French restaurant called Veronique.

When I returned from the Peace Corps—prematurely—I soon moved in with Mandy. We were married a year and a half later, and have been married ever since, and, while I will say more about our relationship a bit later, I want to focus on something else here.

I was disappointed in myself for leaving the Peace Corps early. *Ashamed* of myself would be a truer way to put it. After the years of crew workouts, and the ascetic time alone in Rutland, I thought I could take pretty much anything the world threw at me. But I'd gone into the Peace Corps to help people, and discovered that, on the outer islands, at least, the people didn't really need my help. I had nothing to offer them.

On top of the shame, I'd brought home from the islands an impressive array of illnesses. I had a horrible urinary tract infection, a horrible ear infection. My digestive system was still in shambles from what had been a too-long-untreated bout with intestinal worms. And I'd developed psoriatic arthritis, which plagues me to this day.

I felt like an abject failure. Here I was with an elite education, the exotic U.S.S.R. experience, and friends who were already doing all kinds of remarkable things in the world—in law school and medical school, working on Wall Street, entering the Foreign Service—and I was doing temp jobs two days a week in Boston, unloading trucks for minimum wage, washing dishes, driving a cab. Barely squeaking by, financially.

There were difficulties between me and Mandy, too (she would soon ask to be called Amanda, her actual name and what people call her to this day, so I'll use that name from here on). We'd jumped into living together, having been 'dating' for only about two weeks. And it's hard to overstate the differences between our two upbringings. Her parents, grandparents, and great-grandparents were all college educated. Both her mother's and father's family could trace their heritage back to the Mayflower. The Stearns were an upper middle-class family, with foreign travel experience and a second home. She had four sisters and no brothers. I had two brothers and no sisters. They were Congregational; we were Catholic. They lived in a big house that was filled with antiques and had been built in 1639, and we lived in working-class Revere, surrounded by ordinary furnishings. Her parents would drive around a city to find the least expensive gas; mine would hand me twenty bucks whenever I left the house, even though they had trouble paying the bills. Their dinner-table disagreements were quiet and restrained; ours were loud and raucous. Her father was a lifelong Democrat, my father a lifelong Republican.

We shared a love of spontaneity and adventure, an avid physical connection, an interest in the wider world, and a similar education. We had a great deal of fun, but we also had fights and arguments and silent mornings, and feelings that we might have made a colossal mistake.

So I was sick, broke, ashamed, confused about my future, in love, yes, but in a relationship that had more ups and downs than many have in the sweet early stages. And I was often depressed. One night, walking home from the dishwashing job I despised in Cambridge and which I stayed at for only a single week, I stopped on the bridge over the Charles River, leaned against the concrete rail and looked down. There seemed no point in going on with my life. I was a failure; it was that simple. A quitter. A Peace Corps dropout washing dishes with my fancy education and world travel. I looked down at the dark water and wondered what it would feel like to simply hop over the concrete wall and let myself sink into the cold Charles. There would be something symmetrical about it: dying in the river on which I'd spent so many hours in a crew shell.

I was, in short, feeling very sorry for myself.

And then I felt a certain presence.

Here's the strange thing: feeling sorry for yourself, it turns out, isn't exactly a welcome mat for the helpful spirits of the universe. In fact, self-pity usually acts as a kind of force field that keeps any kind of help at a distance, and so I remain surprised that Elemosina bothered with me in that mood.

Perhaps she was hesitant. I felt the presence, but it was much longer than usual before Elemosina spoke. I stood there in my winter jacket and the work pants that smelled of dirty dishwater, but, instead of looking down at the dark water, I was at least able to raise my eyes and look west up the river. The Charles curls back and forth in that section, with the buildings of Harvard lit up to the right, and Harvard Stadium and the wooden triple-deckers of Allston to the left. I tried to recall some of the best moments on that stretch of river. At Brown, I'd been in a boat that had won a coveted medal in the Head of the Charles Regatta—probably my happiest sporting moment, post-Little-League. In the seat- races for the varsity boat at Boston University, though smaller than all but one of the other oarsmen competing on the starboard side, and therefore at a great disadvantage, I had beaten all of them handily. It sounds like boasting, perhaps, but the truth is, I was a good but never a great athlete, and those positive memories, at that moment, were merely life savers, perhaps literally, an attempt to cling to the few successes I believed I'd had to that point, to remember the fierce part of myself, the part that refused to surrender.

After a time I sensed the familiar presence. Once Elemosina started to 'speak' it was as if my depression instantly evaporated. The future wasn't bright and shining, but at least it wasn't as bleak as it had been a minute earlier. At least there seemed to be reason to go on living.

These are the five pillars of contentment, she began. *1: Good health, including a safe place to live and enough to eat. 2: A harmonious love relationship. 3: Satisfying work. 4: Interior peace. And 5: A clean conscience.*

Of these, you are in possession of only one: number 5. And even that is troubled by the shame and embarrassment you feel at having left the Peace Corps long before your two years were completed.

Let's start with that one first. So much depends upon the angle from which you view life. You can certainly look at your early departure as a grand failure, even a betrayal. Your family arranged for a party to celebrate your departure. You had relatives and friends approach you and congratulate you on what amounted to your willingness to sacrifice the comfort and safety of your life in order to help those less fortunate. Everyone, Amanda included, expected you to be gone for two years. There was a bit of spiritual conceit involved in that, for you. You were making a beautiful gesture, and you were perhaps a bit too proud of it. And, after your time on this and other rivers in those narrow, low boats, and your arduous months in the Soviet Union and alone in Vermont, you believed you could handle any kind of physical or psychological challenge on this Earth. More conceit.

It is a universal law that conceit, or pride, draws trouble. The universe tends toward humility. Not humiliation—though that is sometimes required—but humility. You had to return home and tell family and friends that you'd left the Peace Corps early. And you are embarrassed by that now. Humbled. Even, foolishly, ashamed.

The other way to look at the experience is from a different viewpoint: you tried. You cared enough about the imbalance and injustice in the world to at least attempt to give of yourself and try to alter it. Yes, you were a bit too proud, and yes, you failed. But you were—and are—terribly ill, and you ended up, through no fault of your own, in a situation where you could help no one.

As for Number 4, you're not as bad off as you believe yourself to be on this night. You set a solid foundation for interior piece in Vermont, and you've been pursuing that project, albeit intermittently. Wasn't the Paulist Center Centering Prayer Retreat you attended last month wonderful? You'll remember that all your life.

It's important to keep the proper perspective: interior peace is not a simple matter, not something that can be graphed on a straight line. The brain is extremely complex, a warehouse of every emotion, thought, observation, and experience you've stockpiled for all these twenty-five years, and all the previous lifetimes you've lived. Putting that warehouse in order is a project for many more lifetimes. There will be moments—like the one a few minutes ago—when you feel like an abject failure. During those times, simply hold on. Wait. Don't take action. Try to make yourself tiny in the world. As the world swells up around you, your problems and pain will come to seem somewhat smaller.

But do not be discouraged if your level of interior peace changes with exterior circumstances—bad health, for one. You are not a machine.

I'm going to skip to Number 1). You are currently amid the worst period of bad health you will know for many decades. Again, be patient. Even terminal illnesses have an endpoint, and your troubles, while significant, are far from terminal. It's all part of an in-depth training, one that will go on for millennia—though your suffering will not. You must learn patience at a level you cannot presently imagine. For the time being, simply endure. Do what you can in the way of treatment, and endure.

The same is true of your relationship. You and the spirit that goes by the name 'Amanda'—which means, as you may know, 'beloved'—have, in this life, traveled to this point from vastly different directions. There are bound to be rough spots in each of you that need to be slowly sanded smooth. Persist. As you already know, there are great areas of commonality amid these differences, and real affection. If you both can lovingly work your way through the difficulties, those areas of deep connection will take a larger place in your relationships, and the differences a much smaller one.

In fact, and perhaps I shouldn't tell you this since you are at present so set against becoming a father, but if you and Amanda can overcome these difficult periods, there are two magnificent spirits waiting in another dimension. If the harmony of the relationship suffices, those spirits will be sent to you. It may be the case that you will be offered another kind of spirit to prepare for their arrival, but I can say nothing more on that subject at this time.

Which brings me to the final pillar of happiness: work. You may not feel this right now, but what's happening is that the false thinking that has burdened you for many years is being slowly scraped away. The scraping is painful. To this point, your thoughts about career have been dominated by false motivations. What your parents want you to do. What your schoolmates are doing. What society values: status, money, fame. Beneath these layers of delusion lies your true work. You had a glimpse of it on the beach at Marina del Rey a few years ago, before the Soviet Union, before Micronesia—do you remember?—but there was a thick layer of assumption and obedience covering that truth. Perhaps now you've experienced enough pain, scraped away enough of the falseness, that you can do more than glimpse your true work. You can pursue it. I hope that is the case.

And with those last words—*I hope that is the case*—Elemosina went back to wherever it was she resided, leaving me calmer and more hopeful, but also in a state of utter confusion. I stood for a long time on the dark bridge over the Charles, but there were no longer any thoughts of jumping into the cold river. An idea had been planted in my brain by her words. A seed had been set in soil. In Marina del Rey, on a post-graduate-school cross-country trip with my friend Rick Starzak, I'd borrowed a copy of Hemingway's *A Moveable Feast* from Rick's brother. It's a highly sentimentalized account of the author's early life in Paris, before he'd ever published a novel. He was young and in love, and struggling with money, but he was working hard and building a foundation for his future career. When I finished the book I went out and stood on the dark beach and looked up at the stars and thought I'd finally figured out what I was supposed to be doing with my life: I was meant to write books! After so many months of confusion, there was a kind of exultation in that moment. But then came the job in the U.S.S.R., and the Peace Corps debacle, and I hadn't written a word beyond a few lines of poetry in Rutland, and now I was washing dishes and sick and broke and, on top of everything else, worried about my relationship.

But the next day I bought a BIC ballpoint pen and a pad of lined paper and I began spending every free hour in the Allston Public Library. That was 1978. I wouldn't publish my first novel until 1991, and wouldn't start making a living from my writing until 2000, and even then, of course, there would be setbacks and rough stretches, illness, disappointments, money worries. Still, Elemosina had been right, again: I'd been coming at the question of what to do in this life from the wrong angle, hoping to please my parents, guided by the metrics of society rather than by my own instincts.

In what had really been the darkest hour of my life,

a seed had been planted and watered. I felt like I'd finally come upon the idea for me.

And Elemosina was right about something else as well: it took eighteen more years, but once Amanda and I worked through our differences and deepened our love, we discovered that two magnificent spirits had been waiting to join us all along.

That's where you come in.

Seventh Visit
The Arrival of Other Spirits

Shortly after Elemosina's visit, I quit dishwashing and started driving a taxi in Boston. On the day before I walked into the damp, echoing, shadowy garage on Saint Botolph Street, a driver for that same company had been shot in the back of the head and killed, so there was an element of risk involved. But I loved the freedom of driving cab. At 3:45 in the morning I'd call the company—quietly, so as not to wake Amanda—and ask that a taxi to be sent to 36 Linden Street 'for a driver coming in,' and then I'd stand in the January darkness of the unheated entranceway until the yellow taxi pulled up to the curb. The driver and I would make the ten-minute ride without saying much, but I'd feel a kind of camaraderie with him and I liked the radio patter, the dispatcher relaying calls, "Customer on

Tremont going to the airport. Anybody near 185 Tremont? Come on, ladies and gents, who can help this person catch her plane?" And I liked cruising through the silent, sleeping city.

At the garage, I'd lease my cab for the day, slipping payment through the window where Abe sat with a crowbar for protection and a cigar for company. And then it would be twelve or thirteen hours on the streets, going from neighborhood to neighborhood, stop sign to stoplight, hoping for a long-distance fare and making conversation with clients. Shortly after Elemosina's visit on the bridge over the Charles River, I'd started writing in a serious way, and I'd often take notes or scribble a few lines while I waited in line at the Lenox Hotel or Mass General Hospital.

I drove cab three days a week, and on my off days walked down to the Allston Public Library, found a seat at one of the tables there, took out my ballpoint and white legal pad, and wrote for hours and hours. Maybe thanks to Elemosina, or maybe because I'd tried other things—the exhibit job, the Peace Corps, temp work, dishwashing—and either failed at or felt unsatisfied by them, I'd finally admitted (to myself; I told no one except Amanda about this dream) that what I wanted to do was write for a living. I'd finally managed to shed the expectations of my parents, peers, and society—that I should be a doctor or lawyer, earn a steady paycheck, make enough money to have a beautiful house in the suburbs, build a reputation, be called a professional. Finally and at last, age 25, I'd figured out what *I* wanted to do, and decided that using my time on Earth well was more important than pleasing others. I embraced a big dream, a very big dream—the dream of making a living as a writer —and started to do everything I could to make it reality.

Easier said than done.

It would be twelve long, difficult years from the day I started writing seriously until the day Houghton Mifflin published my first novel, *Leaving Losapas*. In those years, there would be only one funny essay in *Newsweek* and a handful of minor magazine and newspaper publications. You need a massive amount of stubbornness and a very supportive partner to get through twelve years of writing every day, clinging to a dream, and publishing next to nothing. I was fortunate to have both.

In Allston, Amanda continued waitressing, and, along with our housemate, Charlotte, who worked selling fudge in Harvard Square, we were each able to put in our $90 a month for the rent of our two-bedroom apartment with its three-foot-by-eight-foot kitchen and unpredictable heating system. The difficulties of living that way were real, but our time in Allston always had a temporary feel to it, as if something else waited for Amanda and me, somewhere down along a rocky road. We were poor, yes, but we were poor people with excellent educations, and that's a key difference.

That spring, as we were wondering about that rocky road and waiting for the universe to send us a message, Amanda saw a job advertisement for a Spanish teacher at Martha's Vineyard High School, so, taking that as another sign from the Universe, we moved there for one school year. It ended up being the worst year of our life together, to that point, and since. The first month or so wasn't too bad: we rented a ranch house on a cul-de-sac outside Oak Bluffs, at low, off-season rates, and could swim in the ocean until mid-October, and we were married later that month, surrounded by friends and family, in a beautiful ceremony at Brown.

But I'd found work with a middle-aged carpenter who had a terrible temper, and Amanda discovered how little she liked teaching—especially trying to teach Spanish to island-provincial high school kids who had very little interest in the subject—and neither of us was taking home more than about ninety dollars a week. To complicate matters, she became pregnant two months after the wedding, and, while we would have accepted and loved the child to the best of our ability, it would have been a terrible time for us to start a family. In April, just shy of the halfway mark of her pregnancy, we were hit and nearly killed by a drunk driver, and she miscarried a few weeks later.

Near the end of that school year, when we'd both decided we'd had enough of Island life, glamorous as it's made out to be, I saw an ad for a crew coaching job at Williams College. Another sign from God? We finished up on the Vineyard, bought ten-speed bikes with the last of our savings, and spent most of the summer making a thousand-mile bicycle trip around New England, riding fifty miles a day loaded down with gear, paying a few dollars each night for a place to pitch our tent (and sometimes pitching it for free in out-of-the-way places like the Williams College football field), cooking the simplest meals over a campfire. We rode from my parents' house to her parents' house—Revere, Massachusetts, just outside Boston, to central Connecticut, then all the way up the Berkshires to Lake Champlain, and then diagonally southwest over to the coast of Maine and back to Revere. There were many fine moments on that trip, gorgeous scenery, a life outdoors, plenty of exercise, but we've never argued more than we did on those long, arduous days, where every decision had to be made in concert, and we were together constantly.

Our marriage survived the bike trip, and that September we moved to Williamstown, Massachusetts, a college town in the state's northwest corner. The crew coaching job turned out to be, not low-paying, as I'd been led to believe, but completely unpaid. The head coach and I got along about as well as a mean dog and a nasty cat, and I put an ad in the local paper for handyman work even though I had no vehicle and next to no tools or skills. Amanda waitressed at a breakfast place at first, making very little in tips, then upgraded to dinner and lunch shifts at a fancier restaurant. We lived in a freezing apartment because we couldn't afford the electric heat, and slept on the floor because we couldn't afford a bed. We walked two miles to the supermarket once a week to do our food shopping. My back problems grew worse.

During our second year in Williamstown (a.k.a. "The Village Beautiful"), we moved across the street to a warmer but even smaller apartment and things began very slowly to improve. A regular customer at the restaurant saw Amanda going through her contact sheets in a quiet hour and offered her the chance to apply for a job as the photographer at the prestigious Sterling and Francine Clark Art Institute. Amanda got the job. My handyman business grew, if very slowly. I learned as I went and formed the practice of buying a new tool every time I got paid for a job. I put together furniture from kits, painted garages, repointed the mortar in old foundations, replaced panes of glass. Shortly after the accident on the Vineyard, our car had been declared a total loss, but my father found me an old Sears van at auction for a few hundred dollars, so we had wheels again.

In time, thanks to a small amount of savings, money from our wedding gifts, and a very generous first-time-buyer's interest rate, we were able to buy a house across the border in Vermont for $40,000. The house was not very attractive, a simple chalet, four rooms and a shaky deck, two miles down a dirt road. But we were thrilled to finally have our own place. My handyman/carpentry business was doing pretty well by then, though my back problems had worsened and I knew that, sooner or later, I'd have to have surgery. Amanda loved her job at the Clark. We had friends, a little spending money, satisfaction at work, and a place—however modest—to call our own. At the end of a day of carpentry, I'd come home and, after eating a dinner Amanda cooked, and washing the dishes we'd used, I'd go down into a corner of the unfinished basement where there was a four-foot stretch of old countertop and a chair, and I'd write by hand until I was too tired to go on. One of my carpentry customers, an eccentric, book-loving ex-Marine named Michael Miller became my mentor. He recommended books and films, read and critiqued my amateurish pages, met with me every week for a beer and pizza, and hiked the steep hills with me, talking about writers and writing. This went on for several years. Michael kept telling me what I so desperately wanted to hear but did not quite believe: that I had a chance at a writing career, that it could be done, that, in my early thirties, it wasn't too late to get published. Once I admitted my dream to them, two other writer friends—Peter Grudin and Dean Crawford—helped me in various ways, Peter lending me his only computer and getting me into the Williams writing center when I was recovering from back surgery, and Dean introducing me to his agent, who eventually took on and sold my first book.

But, as difficult as the back troubles were, and as important as the writing was, there is another part of our story I want to focus on here. Before buying the house, Amanda and I had helped start a food co-op across the border in Williamstown, and had made friends there. Two of those friends, David Fowle and Helen Olshever, also lived in Pownal, about a twenty-minute, dirt-road walk from our chalet. One winter day, when we'd been in Pownal only a year or so, they invited us over for tea and cookies, and I remember that, as we were walking along the road, Amanda and I were talking about the idea of having a pet. I don't really know why we got onto that subject, because I didn't want a pet. I loved dogs, had grown up with them and had always loved them, but they were so much work, and, whenever we could scrape together the money, Amanda and I liked to travel, so it seemed to me, to both of us, that owning a pet would be foolish.

David and Helen lived in a small geodesic dome they'd built themselves, a kind of comfortably furnished igloo. We were sitting there, enjoying tea and conversation, when a dog appeared out of nowhere, as if part of a magic trick, as if some spirit somewhere had overheard our conversation. I don't remember if the dog scratched at the door and David let him in, or if it had been there when we arrived, but almost as soon as it entered the main room, the dog—large and stately, he'd turn out to be an even mix of Doberman and Black Labrador—came over and sat very close beside me. I began to pat the top of his head and then, since he seemed to enjoy that, to scratch behind his floppy ears. Whenever I stopped, the dog would lift a heavy paw onto my thigh, dig his nails in, and urge me in no uncertain terms to keep going. It was, I suppose, his way of speaking, as if he were trying to say, "Don't stop the scratching, pal. Look at me. I'm here to change your life."

"What a great dog," I said.

David smiled. "That's Jasper. He lives in the doghouse on your road, but really doesn't belong to anybody these days. Want him?"

That was how Jasper came to live with us. He was a magnificent creature, beautiful to look at with a shining black coat and a Doberman's golden accents, smart as a Doberman and affectionate as a Lab. In the mornings, he'd scratch the back door to go out, and trot a mile down to the doghouse where he used to live, and he'd gather his pack there. For the rest of the day, he and his canine associates would roam the woods, fields, and farmland of that part of southern Vermont, looking for adventure and food. Kind as he was, Jasper loved to chase animals. Once, when he and I were out on a walk, I saw him kill a hedgehog with one bite to the back of the neck. He chased deer and bear and turkey and squirrels and racoons, basically anything that moved along the ground. He was the undisputed leader of the pack. In the late afternoon, I'd stop near the doghouse on my way home from a carpentry job, yell out his name, and he'd come loping out of the trees and leap up into the passenger seat of the used blue Dodge pickup I'd bought after selling my van. On weekends, we'd take him for a ride, or walk along the road with him. We never needed a leash. He'd run ahead a hundred feet, then trot back to check in with us, make sure we were all right, then run ahead again, exploring.

We had Jasper for ten years, bringing him with us when we moved from Pownal to the hills of western Massachusetts, ninety minutes southwest. In 1987 we were called back to work in the USSR on the same exhibit program, and we left him in the capable, kind hands of another friend, Bill Press, who rented our house for a year. On the first night without us, confused, lonely, feeling abandoned, Jasper ran away. Bill found him sleeping in a doghouse a mile down the road. I remember so well the day we returned from that job. We drove up to the house. Bill met us at the door. I was anxious to see Jasper again, to see if he remembered us, but Bill said Jasper was out exploring. So I stood out in the front yard and yelled out his name the way I always had in Pownal, "Jass-PER!" Two seconds later he came bounding out of the woods for a festival of hugs and licks and kisses.

Amanda and I had been married for fifteen years by then, and I'd believed, all that time, that I didn't want to have children. Just as I had believed that I didn't want a dog. Jasper changed all that. He made us realize—this was all subconscious, mysterious, never spoken about or even understood until much later—that we wanted other spirits in our life, in our home, and that, even with our love of travel, we could find a way.

Many other things happened in those years. Amanda had found work at the Historic Deerfield Museum, closer to home. I'd published a second novel. The writer Joe McGinniss—whom I'd met when I did repairs on his house in Williamstown—recommended me for a teaching job at Bennington College and I accepted it on the sad day we had to end Jasper's life. We had two incomes and no children, so we traveled some. I designed—and Amanda and I built with our own hands (and the help of friends)—an addition that doubled the size of our simple cape in the hills. From time to time we had family issues and money issues (I taught only half-time at Bennington, and there was a stretch of five years where I couldn't get a third novel published) but we made new friends in the area and kept our old friends, and were content.

And then one day, three years after Jasper died, Amanda and I were lying in bed upstairs in our new addition, and she surprised me by saying, "Rol, I think I'm pregnant." We'd been married seventeen years by then.

"You've thought that before," I said. "Wait a few days and—."

"I bought the test kit," she said, surprising me a second time.

"Okay. Take the test tomorrow and you'll see. We've been here before."

"I want to take the test now," she said. A third surprise.

"Okay, sure, go ahead."

She got out of the bed and went into the bathroom, and I was lying there, alone in the darkness when Elemosina paid her seventh visit.

"Many people believe," she said, *"that if they were only in full control of their lives, if only the world spun according to their wishes, they'd be ecstatically happy. When a person wants something very badly and that something doesn't come into their lives, they are often miserable. And the reverse is also true: when a person doesn't want something, and that something comes into their lives, they often resist vehemently. The greatest Zen monks have an expression: "Say yes to everything." How impossible that seems in bad times! Yes to everything! Yes to death, cancer, professional failure, hunger, disease, divorce, and the other ravages of this Earth! Who would ever agree to such a thing?*

But it turns out the monks are, on one important level, absolutely correct. I'm not speaking of living a passive life, or not trying for what you believe you want. I'm saying only that this trying, this ambition, these wishes, need to be perfectly balanced with the practice of acceptance. Of saying yes. It often turns out that what you think you want would, in fact, make you unhappy, and what you believe you don't want is the key to your happiness and growth.

Let me remind you of what may have seemed a trivial moment in your life. You were driving your truck up to the State Park to have a walk there, remember? Jasper was beside you on the front seat of your pickup. At the entrance, you stopped and paid your fee, and, noticing the creature in your passenger seat, the uniformed attendant there said, "Dogs have to be on a leash."

You nodded, but as you drove away from the booth, you said to Jasper, as a joke, "She thinks you're a dog!"

Do you remember? He was a dog, of course, in one sense—though it's important to remember that you, and almost all human beings, see reality through a very clouded lens. In another, more important sense, Jasper was a teaching spirit who came to you in order to make you understand that your fierce resistance to having children was, in fact, your greatest error.

Even as I'm speaking to you, I can already sense you realize that. You are hoping Amanda comes back to bed and tells you the test is positive, that she is with child. You are ready, you are both ready. This child—there will be two of them, in fact, so let me say instead "these children"—will constitute your greatest joy in this incarnation. There will be difficulties; there always are. But the joy will by such a large measure exceed those difficulties that you will always remember this moment, her return to your marriage bed with the news.

It's often the case that prospective parents will worry about their capacity for parenthood, and worry, too, about the financial responsibilities. Both concerns are real. And now I will remind you of another point in your past, just to emphasize the connectivity of all things, the way seemingly inconsequential incidents and experiences are as essential to your growth as the large moments.

In your senior year you took an essay-writing course at Brown and you were careless about doing the reading. What was wrong with you then?

She seemed, for once, to require an answer, so I spoke the truth: "I don't know. I was lazy, I guess. Distracted. Immature."

There was a long pause before she continued. *But then, a few years later, you were wise enough to carry with you to Rutland several of those books that you'd merely skimmed. One of them was written by another great spirit, Martin Buber. His book,* I and Thou, *dense and difficult as it was when you finally decided to read it, should be one of your primary guides in fatherhood.*

What was he saying in that book? His main idea was to learn to see everyone—every one—as a full human being, and to attempt to treat them accordingly. To see their glory as you feel your own. To see their pain as you feel your own. Their fears, their worries, their aspirations.

That is precisely what you must do with your children. They are neither pets nor possessions, and of course they require care and a certain degree of parental guidance. But they arrive as full spirits. Remember that.

Obviously, you and Amanda are, to use a common phrase, 'the adults in the room.' There will be countless decisions that you, not the children, must make. At the same time, it is the essential aspect of good parenting that you recognize these two souls as full human beings. When they are six months old and waking you up at night. When they are two and beginning to talk back, to push back. When they are twelve and fourteen and sixteen and feeling their way toward adulthood. When they are young women making decisions that might upset you.

This doesn't mean that you 'say yes to everything' in the sense of never disagreeing with them, never advising. You needn't allow a four-year-old to determine what hour she goes to bed, for one good example. But it does mean that you strive always to see the full humanity in them, even when that fullness is a promise and not yet a reality. Respect them in that way, always. See them in that way. And all shall be well."

That was the only time one of Elemosina's visits was cut short by someone other than herself. In this case, it was Amanda leaving the bathroom with quiet footsteps, and then the feel of her climbing onto the mattress beside me and arranging herself under the sheet. She leaned her body close to mine, warmth to warmth. I was still half caught-up in what Elemosina had been saying when I heard these words, "The test was positive, Rol."

And I was happy.

The Eighth Visit
The Miracle of Being

Amanda gave birth to that child when she was 41, and then a second daughter when she was 45 and they are your mother or aunt. Your grandmother then decided she did not want to go back to her museum photographer job. That decision made me happy because, for my whole adult life I've made a practice of trading financial security for freedom, and because I'd hoped that Amanda and I could raise our child together, both of us present, both doing the work, both reveling in the mystery and joys, and meeting the challenges.

That trade—financial security for freedom—would certainly describe the next twenty years for us. I had published two books before Alexandra was born in December of 1997, but the second of those two had been 'orphaned' when my wonderful editor, Alan Williams, left Grove Press. Grove was then swallowed up by Atlantic, and I moved to Little, Brown. My editor there, Tracy Brown, was fired the day the book came out, and the sales of that second novel, *A Russian Requiem,* were awful.

Those poor numbers put my whole writing career—and a decade and a half of work—in jeopardy. Fortunately, after five worrisome years, another highly-regarded editor, Michael Naumann of Henry Holt, made an offer on my third novel, *Revere Beach Boulevard,* almost exactly a month after Alexandra was born. I won't go into too much detail about my publication history, which, like that of a lot of professional authors, is mottled. But when *Boulevard* was accepted, Amanda and I decided, on the basis of the $40,000 advance, that we'd take our new daughter to Italy for a month. That would be the pattern for the rest of our childrearing life: foolish decisions from a financial perspective that were maybe not foolish at all from a life perspective, or even from a parental perspective.

Alexandra (who'd soon become Zan or Zanny and keeps that name into adulthood) was less than four months old when we boarded a plane for Italy. We flew to Rome and rented a car there. Driving in Italy is difficult even on a full night of sleep, but I can't sleep on airplanes, and Amanda had been nursing and hadn't slept much either. We drove tiredly up Italy's west coast, finally giving into our exhaustion and stopping for a nap in the car on the outskirts of the beautiful small city of Montefiascone. An hour's rest there all three of us. And then we were on the road again. But the tiredness and jetlag hadn't been conquered. We passed a sign: *Locanda Rosati, Agriturismo,* made a U-turn a bit farther down the road, and spent the night in a country inn that we've ended up returning to again and again in our many Italian trips.

My salient memory from that trip comes from the next morning. We'd had the typical Italian breakfast—cappuccino, pastry, fruit—and had packed up and were getting ready to leave, when Alexandra threw up all over herself. Giampiero Rosati, the Locanda's owner then and now, laughed happily, said, "*E rigurgitata tutto!" She threw up everything!* as if Zan had just spoken her first full sentence. A perfect stranger, he immediately went to fetch a towel and helped us clean up. From that moment we decided that Giampiero must be an angel, and nothing in our subsequent ten visits to his country inn has made us think otherwise.

We'd rented an apartment in the walled city of Lucca. The weather there, in the words of one local, was *brutto.* Ugly. But we loved that month. I worked on the page proofs of *Revere Beach Boulevard,* Amanda took photos, and we bundled up our precious daughter and walked big loops on top of the wide, sixteenth-century wall. We'd often eat out for lunch—Lucca has some of the best food in a country of great food, and I'd managed to wrangle a food article assignment for the *Boston Globe* to help with the trip's expenses—and Amanda would cook dinner. We'd eat our evening meal with Zan spread out on the dining room table, cooing happily or sleeping, or asking, in the language of infancy, to be fed or changed.

It was, as I said, the beginning of a pattern. During the next twenty years, we took Alexandra to Rome with my mother along for the ride, then, after Zan's sister, Juliana, was born three and a half years later, we took both girls to a chilly place called Contigliano, north of Rome, and, much farther south to Lecce, in the heel of the boot. Thanks to another book advance, this one from Zach Shisgal at Simon and Schuster for *The Italian Summer,* we spent a marvelous season on the western shore of Lake Como in 2007, the girls making friends in the pool we shared with four Italian families. We took hikes, made day trips to Milan and St. Moritz, rode the ferry back and forth across the lake, and sampled every local restaurant we could find.

There were plenty of North American trips, too. Zanny was diagnosed with cystic fibrosis when she was three years old, so, for several years we took her out of school in February, when the classroom is a cold and flu factory, and spent a month on Miami Beach. That, too, was financed by writing work, in this case a week teaching at Dennis Lehane and Sterling Watson's conference, Writers in Paradise, on the other side of the state.

The girls traveled with us for most of the research for *Breakfast with Buddha, Lunch with Buddha,* and *Dinner with Buddha,* trips that took us from Massachusetts to North Dakota, from Seattle to North Dakota, and then from North Dakota to Las Vegas. They learned to play golf at a modest, nine-hole club up in the hills near our home, and we'd drive down to South Carolina for spring vacation and stay at a golf resort there for a week.

Amanda and I loved being parents. It helped that we'd been married for eighteen childless years, had traveled extensively, worked in the USSR for twenty months, been to a hundred movies and gone out to eat countless times. We were old enough to appreciate how quickly the years would pass, so we spent every minute we could with our girls, attending almost all their sporting events and music and ballet performances. Sometimes both of us would separately show up at the end of the grammar school day, because we were off on different errands and both of us wanted to pick up the girls. When Zan and then Juje attended Phillips Exeter, we'd make the two hour and forty-five-minute drive sometimes two or three times a week, not to helicopter over them, just to see them, to cheer them on, to applaud for them, to comfort them in rough weeks when there was a headlice infestation or the strains of the heavy Exeter workload weighed heavily on them.

We weren't rich, not at all—both girls had full scholarships at Exeter and we found ourselves in debt on many occasions—but we somehow managed to live like rich people, and we always made spending time together the priority. One of my books, *American Savior,* was published in Brazil, and the publisher invited me down for a week in Rio. But the girls were ten and seven then, and there was no way to take them along, so I politely refused the offer. Amanda, of course, had made a similar decision—time with the girls over career—and, though I asked her every year or so, she never expressed an urge to return to paid work, except for the occasional wedding photography job.

We had our difficult moments; of course we did. But not many. Maybe because of all the time we gave them, the girls weren't filled with anger when they reached adolescence, and we had the absolute minimum of the types of teenage scenes people had warned us about.

Zan, who'd missed a year of school because of P.O.T.S., a terrible illness, went off to Italy for the second half of her sophomore year in high school, and lived for six months in a family of total strangers. Both girls went away for their last two years of high school. Helicopter parents don't let that happen.

Travel was a refrain in their upbringing—to Italy, in particular, and now both of them love to travel.

Again, this is meant as one example of how to raise kids, not necessarily one that will be right for you. I want to be careful here. First of all, I'm not boasting: every parent chooses what sacrifices to make, and our choosing time with the girls over financial security wasn't exactly heroic. And, secondly, I understand that it's impossible for most middle-class parents to do what we did. It's extremely difficult, often impossible, for American families to survive on a single income, especially a writer's income. We made some tough decisions, yes, and Zanny's health problems (ten sinus surgeries, P.O.T.S., and countless infections by the time she was twenty years old were an enormous burden on her, especially, and on the rest of us, as well) but we were extraordinarily fortunate and I'll never stop being grateful.

All this leads me to Elemosina's eighth visit, and I find it strange, thinking about this now, that she never visited us when the girls were being raised. Maybe I was too busy to 'hear' her, though I doubt that very much. Maybe she sensed I was doing what I should be doing and didn't need her intervention. Certainly those were the busiest and, in many ways, happiest years of my life, but I still wonder why Elemosina stayed absent for more than two decades.

Above, I almost wrote 'eighth and final visit', but I don't know yet that it was the final visit. I won't know that until my last breath, though I find myself anticipating—hoping—that she'll speak to me at some point in my last hours.

By 2023, the girls were 25 and 21. Zan was married, living in Colorado, and the online writing business she'd started was thriving. Juje was a junior at Brown University, living happily in an off-campus apartment with three Jewish boys, two of whom kept kosher. We'd raised them to be confident and considerate, and they'd grown into the most marvelous young women, independent, generous, brave, curious, compassionate, comfortable with themselves and others. Amanda and I were slowly getting used to the empty nest, at peace with that new stage of life, though missing the old days when the four of us ate almost every evening meal together and took all those great trips.

Amanda's sister, Sarah, invited her to go to New Zealand, and, not a fan of lengthy plane rides, I encouraged her to go alone. Not long after she set off, I made a shorter trip to Italy—for the first time by myself.

I rented a three-room apartment in the small city

of Rapallo on the Ligurian coast. On earlier trips, we'd spent time along that coastline—in Genoa and Santa Margherita, in Cinque Terra, in Imperia—but never in Rapallo. I chose it because there was a golf course there, right in the city, and because it was near the coast, and because Liguria has a mild micro-climate and the winter weather isn't *brutto* at all. And mainly because Amanda and I, approaching our seventies now, were looking for a place where we could escape the long New England winters, and Rapallo seemed like one possible option.

In all our Italian trips, I'd been the one providing the money and doing the driving, and Amanda had become expert at all the logistical planning—flights, lodging, car rentals, tickets. I felt that I needed to learn to do those things, rather than so constantly depending on her, and so I downloaded the proper apps and made most of the arrangements, and managed to actually arrive at my destination without any major trouble.

Rapallo was colder than I'd expected, high forties and low fifties for most of the month I spent there. The people weren't nearly as outgoing and friendly as southern Italians, so I didn't have as many opportunities to speak the language I loved. But I enjoyed the solitude, enjoyed learning to cook simple meals for myself and make train arrangements. Some days I'd stay in the apartment most of the time, writing and meditating, going out only for lunch and some exercise. Other days I'd make the hourlong walk up the coast to Santa Margherita and have a meal there at a place I liked, where the waiters were friendly and the *spaghetti alle vongole* and white wine were superb. Or I'd walk the other way, to the northwestern edge of the city, hard against the hills, and meditate in a beautiful old church that was always open and invariably empty.

I played golf only twice, in part because of the cool weather, and in part due to the cost of golf club rentals, and both times sat down afterwards with my Italian playing partners and talked about life there and here.

The apartment was cold at times—only in the high fifties some days—and I had the rare, for me, experience of moments of loneliness, but Italy did for me during that cold January what it had done for me since the 1990s: it offered a slightly different way of looking at life: family, food, and fun sitting a notch higher on the priorities scale than income, industriousness, and incentive. A beautiful *cortesia* on the streets, with people glad to help if you asked and, the rest of the time letting you be.

Of all Elemosina's visits, the one in Rapallo came at perhaps the most ordinary of moments. That day I'd done my back exercises, showered, shaved, walked down to the bakery for a piece of cheesy focaccia and enjoyed it with strong coffee and slices of apple. A meditation, some writing work at the kitchen table. For lunch I headed back through the city and made the long walk northwest along the shoreline road. There was a sidewalk the whole way, and some fairly steep climbs that, at the top, offered spectacular views along the Ligurian shoreline, with green promontories angling down into the bluest water imaginable.

Amanda and I and her sister, Sarah, had spent a wonderful week in Santa Margherita in the summer of

1996—our last trip before the girls arrived—and I took some photos of the *trompe l'oiel* building facades and the gravel shoreline and sent them off toward New Zealand. The *spaghetti alle vongole* was as good as ever, the pasta cooked the way I liked it—*chewy,* the girls had called it when they were young—the small clams were sweet, and it all went perfectly with a cold glass of Vermentino. I took a bus back to Rapallo, then walked the last mile or so up the busy main street, jiggled the key in the temperamental lock on the building's front door, and climbed the three flights of marble steps to my apartment.

In the tile-floored living room there was a red couch, fairly comfortable, that faced across the narrow waist of the room and out through floor-to-ceiling windows. Beyond the windows stood a balcony I never used for more than a few minutes at a time on those cool January days. I sat on the couch and looked out through the windows, above the busy street, to the apartment building across the way. Like most buildings in that city, like most buildings in Italy, it had a red tile roof. There was a single seagull on that roof. For some reason, I stood up, went to the window, and watched the seagull step across the tiles, jabbing its beak down from time to time to snatch some invisible piece of food, but mostly just parading up there, prancing, head up, gray wings tucked close. I watched it for a long time. At first, I had the thought that its life must be boring: no activities like golf or language lessons, some variety in terms of food and a little travel, but nothing like the variety of opportunities available to a human being.

But then it occurred to me that the seagull might be experiencing life in a way very different from the way I experienced it. The bird might be feeling the simple fact of *being* in a way my overcrowded, overly busy mind did not allow me to feel. What if it went through the hours unworried, just *experiencing the fact of life in this world?* Feeling it fully, deeply, continuously. The smell and texture of the air, the clouds and sky and all the roofs and sidewalks where it might land, the sound of the surf against the gravelly downtown beach. I watched and watched, trying to feel the world that way. . . and then, for the eighth time, I sensed the amazing presence.

It has taken you a long while to reach this point, Elemosina said, in what sounded to me like a pleased tone. *All these decades of meditation and marriage. All the reading of books from various religious traditions. All that questioning and pondering. All that suffering and pleasure. All those mistakes, if we can use that term. All the exhilaration and challenge of raising the two special souls you call your daughters.*

I know that you've read the account of the Zen student who, after many years of arduous training still hadn't experienced enlightenment and so was asked to leave the monastery. He settled in the town and lived a simple life. One day as he was sweeping the walk in front of his rented house, he brushed away a piece of gravel and heard it strike the stone wall, and that sound, that tink, *let him understand, finally, what all the hours of hard practice in the Zendo hadn't shown him.*

I know you've read about Thomas Merton,

traveling in what was then called Ceylon—now Sri Lanka—and approaching the great statue of the reclining Buddha on Polannaruwa. You memorized his brief comment about that moment in The Asian Journal.

Those were both simple, ordinary moments, but weren't the results extraordinary? You found the accounts puzzling, though, didn't you?

Most puzzling of all was Jesus's famous statement, which you heard so often as a boy: I am who am.

What could that possibly mean, you wondered.

And now, I think, you are beginning to know the answer.

In many places in your writings you've talked about the habit of taking life for granted, of not fully appreciating the miracle of being. *You sensed that there was some other level of appreciation, of awareness, and, like countless others, you had many, many moments of that deeper appreciation. Sometimes just lying in bed at night, with the tasks and pleasures of the day behind you, you were able to feel, in the darkness and silence, another kind of aliveness. Sometimes after a cold swim you would feel it. In Rutland, walking the snowy golf course, and in quieter moments in the Soviet Union. You sensed it (and this is not common) both times when your lovemaking with Amanda led to conception, though you've been appropriately discreet about discussing that with anyone but her. Perhaps because you worried no one would believe you.*

Everyone on Earth has similar experiences, these

moments of awakeness, these glimpses of a dimension of the larger truth. Some people—like that Zen student—pursue them; others pay them no heed. Sin—real sin—the harming of another soul, has its own punishment—not by a vengeful, insulted God, but simply by the laws of the universe, which are unbendable—and one part of the punishment is that the mind is blocked off from these moments of awareness. Perhaps that sounds trivial: you harm someone, and then you are kept from feeling the miracle of being alive. But it is actually what condemns you to countless more incarnations, more suffering, more difficulties, eons of them in some cases, until you learn what you must learn. Not a trivial thing at all.

Remember those words: I am who am.

The seagull might say those words if it were able to speak in human language. You are correct in assuming that it feels the miracle, the magnificence, the astonishing fact of life *in a way most humans do not. This is why we call such creatures* 'sentient beings.'

But even that definition is flawed. Trees feel this aliveness. Stones, with their whirling atoms, feel it. It is no coincidence that the only weapon capable of completely ending human life on Earth is fashioned at the atomic level. At that level, that predictable but raucous level which human science has only begun to penetrate, there is continuous aliveness. *The consciousness of* God*—to use a word, as you may have noticed, I try to avoid—exists in those tiny molecules just as much as in the enormous bodies of planets and the 'empty' space between them.*

I am who am.

This 'am' is the point. This awareness of the pure, simple fact of being, the fact to which humans pay so little attention. It is the reason for the long, seemingly senseless meditations in some spiritual circles that involve nothing more than watching the breath go in and out through the nostrils for hours at a time. That is a way of training the practitioners not to take the breath for granted, and so, not to take life for granted.

Harming others, remaining caught up in a mindless and continual search for more and more pleasure, being enamored of constant distractions, pervasive fear or worry or preoccupation with oneself—all those serve to keep us from experiencing our aliveness in the moment.

Strangely, perhaps, both pleasure and pain can lead us to that appreciation. The joy of music, for instance, can lift our awareness. The beauty of a piece of art—dance, sculpture, drama, poetry, prose—can serve that purpose. Time in nature can also awaken us. But pain can, too. What's required is to reject the impulse to flee it immediately. This is what some of the ancient Christian monks understood when they participated in self-flagellation. But they understood it only partly and imperfectly. It's foolish to whip oneself. There's enough pain in life, and if we can try to focus on that pain—when it is not overwhelming—rather than fleeing from it, it can serve the same purpose that the gravel ticking against the stone wall served for the Zen monk. I'm not suggesting you don't make an effort to alleviate pain; you should do so, of course. I'm saying only that, at the moments when you are in pain you should try to pay attention to it, rather than wishing so desperately for it to be gone. Lend your attention, *as the saying goes in both Italian and English. That is the point of fasting, too—an aspect of so many faiths—not to punish yourself or atone for your sins, but to encourage you to appreciate the taken-for-granted act of eating and drinking.*

So, just now, you have touched this dimension in a new way. Intellectually, at least. Remember the heavy stone seagull a friend of your father-in-law gave you and Amanda as a wedding present? You laughed at it and left it behind in the hotel. But you remember it, and you remember the seagulls at Revere Beach when you were a boy, and so now a seagull has come to give you this gift of intellectual understanding of the spiritual puzzles you pondered and could not solve. I find that amusing.

Of course, important as this understanding is, you feel it now mostly at the intellectual level, as I said. For the rest of your time in this body, it will be important to deepen that understanding, to spend more and more time in the simple awareness of being. This doesn't mean sitting endlessly in meditation. Go about your life. Visit with your daughters, write your books, walk, swim, work, sleep, play golf, eat and drink, suffer and enjoy. But try to let all of those activities and moments sharpen your alertness, and remind you that you ARE. *That deepening awareness will lead you to joys you cannot imagine. Trust me.*

And with that, Elemosina, my spirit guide, my divine friend, disappeared forever. Or perhaps only went silent for a time. I went over to the red sofa and sat there watching the light of the day slowly fade. The seagull had abandoned its post on the roof across the way. On the street below, the noise of cars, trucks, and ambulances increased with the evening rush. I could sense streetlights and headlights breaking the darkness. I could hear the engines and tires and sirens. I could smell a meal being cooked in the apartment next door, sweet tomato gravy, it seemed, an aroma from my grandmother's kitchen. My hands were palm-down on my thighs and I could feel the fabric of my pants against my skin. I tried, not to puzzle over Elemosina's words—there would be time for that in abundance—but simply to feel the living moment, and the next living moment, and the next.

After a while, I thought back over her other visits, the long stretch of fifty-eight years between my paternal grandfather's death and this hour in the country where he'd been born, the suffering and pleasure I'd experienced in those decades, the broken back, the birth of my children, the beautiful years with my beautiful wife, the travel and toil, the worry and creativity, the meals, the lovemaking, the friendships, the arguments and disappointments, the achievements and exultations, the raising of our daughters, the writing of books, the walks, the music, the museums, the beauty and ugliness. Life, all of it. Precious in all its manifestations, but its preciousness so often ignored. I vowed then, as the great master Soen Sahn Nim had suggested in a Zen retreat I attended in Providence, Rhode Island after our thousand-mile bike trip in 1980, to 'try, only try.' Try, without being rigid about it, to sharpen my attention, to appreciate all the moments of my life, the plain and the difficult and the joyful, without wishing any of them away.

To appreciate the simple fact of being alive, on this Earth, in this body.

And with that, my dear grandchild, I shall leave you. It's possible we will never meet, and that these pages will serve as our only 'communication', one-sided though it may be. I hope they were of some interest to you, maybe even some value. And I hope your life as is full of adventure and love as mine has been, and that you'll have your own Elemosina who 'speaks' to you from time to time, in whatever form she may take.

One last thing: please give my warmest love to your mother and your aunt. *Arrivederci, Nonno.*

The End

Conway, MA, 6/1/23—Conway, MA, 3/4/26

About the Author

Roland Merullo is an awarding-winning author of thirty books. His works of fiction include: *Breakfast with Buddha,* a nominee for the International IMPAC Dublin Literary Award, now in its 23rd printing; *The Talk-Funny Girl,* a 2012 ALEX Award Winner and named a "Must Read" by the Massachusetts Library Association and the Massachusetts Center for the Book; *Vatican Waltz* named one of the Best Books of 2013 by *Publishers Weekly*; *Lunch with Buddha* selected as one of the Best Books of 2013 by *Kirkus Reviews*; and *American Savior,* a Massachusetts Center for the Book, "Honor Award" winner, *Revere Beach Boulevard* named one of the "Top 100 Essential Books of New England" by the *Boston Globe*; and *A Little Love Story* chosen as one of "Ten Wonderful Romance Novels" by *Good Housekeeping*, and *In Revere, In Those Days* a Booklist Editors' Choice Recipient. *Revere Beach Elegy,* one of his nonfiction titles, was the winner of the Massachusetts Book Award for nonfiction.

Merullo's essays have appeared in numerous publications including the *New York Times, Yankee Magazine, Newsweek,* the *Boston Globe, the Philadelphia Inquirer, Boston Magazine, Reader's Digest, Good Housekeeping,* and the *Chronicle of Higher Education.* His books have been translated into German, Spanish, Portuguese, Korean, Croatian, Chinese, Turkish, Slovenian, Bulgarian, Czech, and Italian. He has been a frequent contributor of commentary for National Public Radio affiliates.

For additional information, please visit: rolandmerullo.com

Some Other Books by PFP/AJAR Contemporaries

***Waking Slow* – Ioanna Opidee**

"*Waking Slow* shines light on not just the extremes of violence, but the more subtle and insidious indignities and inequalities around us. . . .Opidee has given us a sensitive protagonist who walks the uncomfortable, universal line between alienation and acceptance. The book offers a look at what it takes to put the shards back together after a shattering, showing not that it's easy, or fast, but possible."

—Nina MacLaughlin, ***Boston Globe***

Big City Cat: My Life in Folk Rock
- Steve Forbert

"Like his stunning first album, Steve's compelling first book is very much alive on arrival."

—David Wild,
contributing editor, ***Rolling Stone***

Lunch with Buddha
- Roland Merullo

"A beautifully written and compelling story about a man's search for meaning that earnestly and accessibly tackles some well-trodden but universal questions. A quiet meditation on life, death, darkness and spirituality, sprinkled with humor, tenderness and stunning landscapes."

—***Kirkus*** –Starred Review / "Best of 2013"

This Is Paradise: An Irish mother's grief, an African village's plight, and the medical clinic that brought fresh hope to both
- Suzanne Strempek Shea

—Named to ***Yankee Magazines'*** 2014 "New England Wish List."

Smedley's Secret Guide to World Literature **- Askold Melnyczuk**
"A teen, wired more to his phone than the repercussions of his actions [who] is trying to make sense of his life. Melnyczuk captures these existential dilemmas in a believable voice."
—Clea Simon, ***Boston Globe***

Who Do You Think You Are?: Reflections of a Writer's Life
- Joseph Torra
"A memoir about one man's life of writing and self-discovery that flows in a natural way and hums with a sense of honesty." —***Kirkus Reviews***

Visions of Johanna **- Peter Sarno**
"Sarno's beautifully written literary novel concerns an unlikely pairing…The author skillfully portrays Matt, drawing readers into the story with his use of metaphor and lush language…As the story reaches its affecting conclusion, readers may even shed a tear or two."
—***Booklist,*** **starred review**

www.ingramcontent.com/pod-product-compliance
Lightning Source LLC
LaVergne TN
LVHW090520110826
845146LV00003B/932

* 9 7 9 8 9 8 6 6 2 6 6 6 6 *